Overcoming Common Problems

Coping when Your Child has Special Needs

Suzanne Askham

sheldon PRESS

Published in Great Britain by
Sheldon Press
Holy Trinity Church
Marylebone Road
London NW1 4DU

British Library Cataloguing-in-Publication Data

A catalogue record for this book is available from the British Library

ISBN 0–85969–825–4

Typeset by Deltatype Limited, Birkenhead, Merseyside
Printed in Great Britain by
Biddles Ltd, Guildford and King's Lynn

Contents

Acknowledgements   vii
Introduction   ix

1 Realization   1
2 Coping with the medical world   24
3 You and your relationships   39
4 Taking control   55
5 Complementary therapies   73
6 Your older child   93

Appendix 1 Useful organizations   105
Appendix 2 Help with finance and equipment   110
Appendix 3 Further reading   112
Index   115

Acknowledgements

The biggest thanks must go to the many parents and their children I have encountered over the past three years, in hospital waiting rooms and wards, special needs centres, and support groups both national and on-line. Although I didn't realize it at first, in effect these parents and their comments became part of an anonymous, highly informal survey of parental experiences, many of which appear in these pages. Thank you to every parent who unwittingly contributed in this way. As it would have been impossible to ask permission from such a wide-ranging group, all names and confidences have been held back, except where individuals expressly gave permission for quotes to be used.

Particular thanks must go to Annie Cawthorn of the Microcephaly Support Group, Mark Elewitz of the on-line microcephaly group, Steve Moody of the Cranio-Facial Support Group and Elaine Bennett of the Delayed Myelination Group. Also to Sultana Khan, osteopath, and Natasha Lindeman, homeopath, for teaching me a great deal about complementary methods through their skilful treatment of my son. Also to Elaine Gibson, Portage, and Tracy Mabbs, Linda Friar and their colleagues at Montys Nursery for teaching me that to build up a child's skills, you need to concentrate on the really important things, such as confidence and enjoyment of life. And thanks to the many therapists, too numerous to mention, for passing on their knowledge about the importance of sensory issues in a child's development.

Heartfelt thanks, and a glass of wine, to Carolyn Moncur, Emma Hearne, Louise Smallwood and Julie Whiteford for keeping me sane on Fridays. For Joanna Moriarty at SPCK for being so supportive and enthusiastic about publishing this book. And finally, thanks to my family in England and Ireland, for always being so positive and full of encouragement. And most of all to Steven and Timmy, for sharing the adventure.

Dedication

This book is for you and the child or children you are reading it for. May your lives be filled with happiness and health.

Introduction

Can we establish something right away? You, like me, are a normal parent with a normal child ... who just happens to have health problems.

It's worth stressing this at the outset because when a doctor or some other health specialist refers to the fact that your child has special needs, it sounds horrendous. It gives the impression that your family has left the normal world and entered a dismal ghetto where everyone is flawed – and that you'll never get the chance to enter the real world again.

It needs reiterating that you and your child are not flawed – or, at least, no more than anybody else in the world. Everybody has strengths and weaknesses, and a human without any flaws is no human at all.

To give one obvious example, a very large proportion of the British population has imperfect sight and has to wear glasses or contact lenses. Does that mean that all those people have special needs? Most of them would be very cross indeed if you suggested as much! And yet, in a sense, they do.

The moral is, whatever health problem your child may have, try not to let yourself get upset by any 'labels' that are applied. There are an awful lot of these labels, and many of our children get more than one.

Your child, for example, may be given a general label such as 'special needs', 'disabled' or 'learning difficulties'. More specifically, he or she may be given specific diagnoses, such as 'autism', 'cerebral palsy', 'Down's syndrome' or 'attention deficit disorder'. And they may be given descriptions such as 'failure to thrive' or 'hypertonia', which just means high muscle tone.

Labels are a convenient way of grouping similar children together, and they do have their uses. Doctors find such labels useful because it gives them a basic idea of suitable tests and treatment. Likewise, parents may get a great deal out of joining a national support group for their child's particular diagnosis (that is, label), because it's very helpful to talk to others who know exactly what you're going through.

But within any label, or diagnosis, whether it be autism, Down's syndrome, dyslexia or whatever, there is enormous variation, because we are all individuals. Labels, though, can actually be harmful, because they can place restrictions on a child's potential.

However, many children never get a definite diagnosis, because they don't fit any known label sufficiently well. With these children there's clearly a problem, such as developmental delay or a learning difficulty, but the reasons for it are never clear. In some ways this can be an advantage.

Let's consider my own son, Timmy, who is three and a half years old. He is delightful, bright, affectionate, full of curiosity, a bit of a madcap. He has low muscle tone, can't yet walk, has limited speech, and various other delays.

In Timmy's case, as with many other children, countless tests have identified no specific cause for his health problems. From time to time he has osteopathic treatment, which I value highly.

One day, I was talking to the osteopath about the doctors' continuing quest for a diagnosis, a label. The osteopath shook her head, half-exasperated, half-laughing. 'He has "Timmy Syndrome",' she said. By that, she meant that he is just himself, with his own unique blend of strengths and weaknesses. We can encourage him in all areas, but we would be doing that whether he had a label or not.

I don't know what your child's exact situation may be, but I do know that your child is first and foremost an individual. Yes, there are problems, otherwise you wouldn't have picked up this book. These could be very mild – a developmental delay or behavioural problem that will sort itself out in the next six months or so. Or they could be serious: a debilitating illness or condition that means leading a normal life is unlikely. Alternatively, the problems could be somewhere in between.

But whatever the problems, there is a lot you can do to make life better for your child, yourself, and your whole family.

One thing you *can* be sure of is that you are not alone. There are many, many families in your situation. Government figures show that one in five of all school-aged children are classified as having special needs at any one time.

Likewise, every parent of a child with special needs has been through agonies of worrying and soul-searching. 'Was it something I did?' we wonder. 'Am I doing the right thing now? How will my child cope in the future? How will I tell people without crying? How will I cope with other people's comments? How will I get through the next medical appointment? Why did this have to happen to me?'

All parents wish, again and again, that they didn't have to be in this situation. And facing up to the fact that we are, that there is no getting away from it, can take many months.

This is all entirely normal; it's part of the psychological process of adjusting to a new reality. You have to let go of your old assumptions about how life is supposed to be. In its place, you develop a more realistic view.

In fact, the experience can actually – though you may find this hard to believe right now – bring you benefits. You become more understanding of other people's problems, whatever they may be. You gain a wider perspective of life. And eventually, as the months pass and you find that you are coping, you gain a new strength and confidence that other people will recognize and respect.

This book can be your companion along the way. I've written it because three years ago I really needed a book like this, and couldn't find one. The books I did find on special needs tended to be depressing in the extreme. Some were cold, clinical medical textbooks that looked at symptoms and ignored the child's personality. Others seemed to be rather patronizing to parents.

Over time I did find several good books that gave me interesting insights, enlightened techniques, or encouraging success stories from other parents. These I have listed in Appendix 3: Further reading at the end of this book, along with other sources of information.

You'll find most of the material in this book comes directly from parents' experiences. This is because I have found that parents are the experts – they've lived it, they know what it's like, they've found practical solutions that they can pass on to you. And the good news is that the overwhelming majority of parents cited in this book have found that over time it gets easier – it really does. You, your child with special needs and your family, can all reclaim a normal life. This book will empower you to get the right help and answers.

One of the areas that concerns parents most, especially in the early years, is how to deal with the relentless barrage of medical tests and consultations. Ongoing hospital appointments can be very draining for you and your child.

This book will give you practical ideas on how to make the experience much easier. It will help you to steer your way through endless medical advice, not all of which may seem right for your child. It will help you to choose which tests you feel are appropriate, and to politely but firmly reject the rest. It will help you to choose the best physical therapies and complementary treatments for your child.

On a daily basis, the suggestions in these pages can help you to cope with every aspect of your child's special needs – and your own reactions to the situation. This really does matter, because when you're coping, you feel happier, your child feels happier, and you're making decisions from a position of strength. Other people pick up on this, and respect you accordingly.

Above all, this book should help you to reach the point where you look at your child and simply see a normal, lovable, sometimes maddening, individual, with his or her own unique blend of strengths and weaknesses. Special needs have to be dealt with, but they are just one aspect of family life. This book will help both you and your family to regain a healthy perspective.

And you never know, you might even find that your child ends up confounding the doctors. This happens surprisingly often in my experience – my own son has already done much better than predicted. Confounding the doctors is fun. I'd like to suggest you make yourself a vow today: 'We're going to confound the doctors!'

And never give up hope.

1

Realization

It dawned on us slowly, in the first few months. At four weeks, our son started smiling, which we knew was good. But he was slow to reach all his other milestones. His growth began to tail off. Too much noise upset him. There were lots of little signals that all was not right.

One mother whose newborn baby was whisked straight into special care says she immediately felt she was in a hi-tech nightmare, torn from her baby.

In contrast, one father coped magnificently for the first few days while his son was in special care. He even began to search for information about his son's condition. Then, on the fifth day, he collapsed in tears. But by the time his son was three months old, this particular father was back on track, determined to do everything he could to ensure the best possible outcome for his child.

Another couple only suspected a problem when their son was approaching two. He had developed a lot of strange repetitive habits: he liked to lie on the floor and 'walk up' walls, and he'd open and shut the same door for hours on end if they let him. And when they tried to take him on the bus, or to anywhere noisy, he screamed and screamed.

Other parents realize much later, in the third or fourth year, or not until their child starts school.

Maybe you knew from birth, maybe you didn't suspect a thing until your child went to school and couldn't cope with reading and writing. Maybe, for you, the realization came at some point in between.

We all discover in different ways but, for all of us, one of the earliest indications is an uncomfortable feeling at the pit of our stomach. Something is not as it should be. This feeling is disquieting, even terrifying. 'If there is something wrong with my child,' your thinking goes, 'then there could be something extremely wrong.'

We do not know the extent of the damage. Our imaginations fill in the gaps, upsetting us with imaginary scenarios. Or we refuse to think about it at all, but the worries come out at night in upsetting dreams, or a feeling of tension, of being unable to speak about anything normally.

It can affect the way we are with our partners, children, other relatives and friends. Even when we're trying not to think about it, it can dominate our thoughts so that we feel we're caught up in a nightmare. It can affect everything we do and think.

In the early stages, there is probably a sense of numbness, of shock. We may also feel very isolated, as though everyone else in the world is normal – except us. (This isn't true, of course, but it's how we feel.)

Our feelings are powerful at this early stage, and they are going to continue to be powerful over the weeks and months ahead. Letting your feelings out, talking about them with friends, relatives or other parents in the same situation, even writing them down, are all vital steps towards coping.

Many parents feel a sense of bereavement, a sense of loss. They may grieve the loss of the child they thought they had, or were going to have. Or they grieve over the normal lifestyle they thought they would enjoy, instead of the one they actually have, which appears very different and bleak.

Many parents feel anger, which may be directed at doctors and other health professionals, education officials, other parents, their partners, or even themselves. Sometimes parents can get stuck in anger for months or years on end.

And sometimes there can be a feeling of denial: 'This isn't happening, there's nothing wrong with my child', which may alternate with the opposite extreme: a sense of absolute hopelessness, as though nothing will ever improve.

When you're in these early stages of realization and reaction, it is extremely difficult to imagine yourself in a situation where you can accept and love your child just as he or she is, and have the energy and wherewithal to create the best possible upbringing.

But you will eventually reach that state, I promise you. It may help to compare this emotional wound to a physical blow – the process of pain and healing is remarkably similar. First, there is a feeling of shock and numbness, followed by sharp pain. Then comes the bleeding, the clotting, the bruising. The soreness and the bruising are extremely uncomfortable, but they are actually signs of the body healing itself.

And so it is with emotional pain. The numbness, pain, fear, anger, tears and denial are all useful stages on the road to coping. That's why it's important to listen to these feelings, because then we don't get stuck in particular stages. If you do feel you are stuck in a particular emotion, you will find many strategies throughout this book that may help you to move on.

Unfortunately, many of us find we don't have time to deal with our feelings, or even start thinking straight, because the medical/educational 'special-needs conveyor belt' has started up. Your child is suddenly on it and you are running to keep up. You do not feel in control. You do not feel that you ever will be again. But you will. Just read on.

Sometimes doctors tell us there is a problem before we acknowledge it to ourselves – although I think, even then, most of us had suspected, deep down. There's no getting away from that feeling at the pit of your stomach that all is not right.

Occasionally doctors inform us of the situation and we *don't* have a corresponding uncomfortable feeling in our stomachs. Trust your feelings – the situation is probably not as bad as the doctors are telling you.

Sometimes you have to fight to get a referral after you have begun to realize that there may be a problem. The health visitor and your GP try to reassure you, perhaps saying your child will grow out of it. But you can't stop worrying, and eventually you do get referred to a paediatrician.

This feeling of having to fight to get your views taken seriously is one that many parents experience at different stages. 'We have to fight for everything, don't we?' commented one mother of a child with learning difficulties.

But a useful tactic in these early stages is not to think of your situation in such negative terms – even though there's plenty to feel negative about. Instead, try rephrasing it in a positive, proactive way.

Start thinking of yourself and your partner as the primary experts on your child's health. (You are, you know.) Even if right now you feel stumped, and desperate for an expert to tell you what to do, the reality is that *you* are in the best position to help your child.

This is because no one knows your child like you do. You know what makes him happy and what makes him sad; what motivates him and what demotivates him; what foods he likes, and which foods and medicines give him an upset stomach.

Even when your child was just a day old, you knew more about these things than anybody else in the world, because you are one of his parents – as such, you have tuned into him. Being close to him in this way means that you will develop an instinctive sense of what feels right for him, and what feels wrong.

But if by any chance you have had difficulties in bonding with him, don't agonize and worry about this. It's not because you're a bad parent. It's because other things – like medical intervention, or your own fear of losing him – have got in the way. There are easy, daily things you can do to become closer to your child, and you'll find these listed later in this chapter.

Of course, there'll be lots about your child's health care you don't know, but that's where the doctors and other specialists come in. They are there to give you the benefit of their training and expertise. Ultimately, though, you and your partner have the final say.

This means that it's up to you to find the right specialists to back up your hunches, give your child the therapy you feel is necessary. In effect, you, together with your child's other parent, are becoming the leaders of a little team, which is dedicated to caring for your son or daughter.

Who joins your child's team depends ultimately on you. If you want a neurologist and no one else has suggested it, you ask for one. If you want a second opinion, you ask for one. If you're not sure what a particular treatment will mean for your child, you ask for clarification before making a decision to go ahead. If you're not happy with your child's physiotherapist, you ask for another one. If you want complementary medicine in the form of a homeopath, you arrange it.

In the early days it will be hard to think this way. But the sooner you start, the better you will feel. Thinking like this puts you in a powerful, assertive frame of mind.

Of course, it's not necessarily the way the medical profession expect a parent to behave. Traditionally, doctors and other health workers are used to doling out prescriptions and/or advice, and the parents are supposed to agree meekly with everything.

But the reality nowadays is that parents often become extremely well informed about their child's health – we have to be. Our views are to be respected. And ultimately, the doctors, therapists and other health workers on your team will appreciate that attitude, because they know you are taking responsibility for your child's health.

They know you won't do anything you don't feel comfortable with. And if you disagree with something, you will say so. That's reassuring for them: it takes some of the weight off their shoulders.

There's another thing to bear in mind at the start: don't get too grumpy or resentful with medical personnel. If your child is in an emergency situation, perhaps involving life-saving surgery, resentment is less likely to figure: you'll probably be profoundly grateful for the great good that medicine can bring.

But when the problem is harder to define and treat – delayed development, learning difficulties and failure to thrive all come into this category – it's tempting to turn against doctors and other health professionals who, in your view, aren't doing the best they could. If this happens to you, remind yourself that it's better for your child if you all work well together. None of us has all the answers. But together, as a team, we can work wonders. We're all on the same side really.

Hearing the news

Probably the first major step that we all have to face is that initial, nerve-racking session in a consultant paediatrician's room, where you'll be given some kind of prognosis about your child's condition. This is a scary moment, because the doctor's words put the official seal on the situation: you have to admit to yourself that this really is happening.

Doctors break the news in different ways – it can't be easy for any of them. Many are vague, and say, quite rightly, that they cannot predict the future, but that there is much that can be done through therapies to help your child.

Others feel it is their duty to dash any hopes at the outset. This is probably the most misguided approach. How do they know what the future holds? How can any of us know?

Let me give you an example of this based on my own area of experience. One of my son's distinguishing characteristics is microcephaly – which is the Greek for 'small head'. It means that his head is smaller than the heads of 98 per cent of the population. Microcephaly is not really a diagnosis: it's simply a description.

Doctors have always liked using ancient Greek and Latin expressions instead of plain English, because traditionally it impressed patients! But I think it's always a good idea to translate such expressions into plain English, so you can see more clearly what they are talking about.

In itself, having a small head is not a problem, but it may mean that the brain hasn't grown as big as it ought to due to any one of a number of reasons – such as infection in pregnancy; or absence of oxygen at some critical period; or perhaps it's caused by a genetic condition.

If the brain is smaller than it should be, there is unfortunately a greater risk of complications such as sensory processing problems, developmental delays, learning difficulties, feeding problems, failure to thrive, hypotonia, cerebral palsy, quadriplegia, epilepsy, visual impairment, autism. Basically, there's a long, frightening list of things that can go wrong in a child with microcephaly.

I have come into contact with many other parents whose children

5

have microcephaly: both through the Microcephaly Support Group, whose newsletter I produce; and also through an on-line microcephaly parents' group.

Many of these parents report being told early on some really depressing things by their child's doctors: some were told their daughter would never walk; others were told their son would never talk. But eventually most of these children have learnt to walk and talk. Of course, some haven't – the doctors aren't always wrong.

But hearing and reading all these parents' experiences has taught me that the doctors are frequently more pessimistic than they need to be. Recently, there was a brief comment about this subject in *Connections*, the newsletter of the Microcephaly Support Group. I reprint it here because it seems to sum up many parents' experiences:

> It seems every parent has encountered a Doctor Doom. These are the medical experts who feel it their duty to say things like: 'You'll have to face the fact your child may never walk.'
>
> Most parents accept everything their doctors say, at least at first. Then they hear about the on-line support group, write in sadly, and get several replies from parents who say, 'Been there, heard that, but my son is four now and at this moment he's walking about in the kitchen emptying my cupboards.'

The moral is: don't let yourself be affected too much by other people's views on how your child will progress – however expert they may be.

When the diagnosis is obvious

If your child has an immediately identifiable syndrome, this brings advantages and disadvantages all of its own. Perhaps the most obvious example of this is Down's syndrome.

Down's syndrome is the most commonly diagnosed genetic condition. This means that a lot is known about it. It also means that a lot of people will tell you authoritatively what the future is likely to hold for your child. But you have an advantage over every expert: you know your own child better than anyone else. Even in the earliest days, this holds true, because as a parent you tune into your child in a way that no busy health professional ever has time to do. And, as every other parent in your situation will tell you, your child is first and foremost an individual, with his or her own blends of strengths and weaknesses.

Look at it logically. We generally have 23 pairs of chromosomes which, for convenience, we number from 1 to 23. Down's syndrome involves an extra chromosome for number 21, or part of an extra chromosome, so there are three copies of that particular chromosome.

But your child still has 22 other pairs of chromosomes; the Down's chromosome is just a small part of the whole picture. And it's all the chromosomes together that make up the unique individual who is your child.

Unfortunately, we tend to focus on the small percentage of genes that are different. And when we do that, we become pessimistic. We tend to see all the reasons why our child won't do well, and our low expectations may become a 'self-fulfilling prophecy' (in other words, because we *expect* little, little is achieved).

Yet children with Down's syndrome do a lot better today than they used to. They may have a totally average IQ. They can, and do, graduate from university, marry, hold down jobs. These things may be harder for them to achieve – and they're by no means the only recipe for a happy life anyway – but they are possible.

The most important thing, as with any child, is to love your child just the way she is, give her the help to improve weak areas, and encourage the development of her strengths. Believe in your child's potential; don't let low expectations limit her future. It's also vital to build up her confidence and self-esteem by praise and listening.

There are other genetic conditions that can be quickly diagnosed, and many rarer ones that may take longer – or may turn out not to be genetic in origin after all.

Genetics are something of a fashion among paediatricians today. Doctors get very excited about the fact that our entire gene pool is gradually being mapped out. When in doubt, they will often suggest that a child's problems are genetic in origin, when in reality there's no firm evidence to support this.

I realized this on a particularly harrowing day, when no fewer than seven geneticists gathered around my son at Great Ormond Street Hospital to examine him in detail. I wasn't sure whether to laugh or cry. It made me think of one of those jokes: how many geneticists does it take to change a light bulb?

They were a likeable bunch, and they explained that they preferred to go around in a 'gang' because that raises the chances of spotting a genetic condition. But to me it seemed a bit overwhelming, and at the end all seven could only say what geneticists everywhere spend a lot of time saying: 'Well, it's possible that he has a genetic condition, but actually we don't know.'

If your child does have a definite, or suspected, genetic condition, this can feel very damning, like an immutable life sentence. After all: we are all stuck with our genes.

But even here I suggest you adopt a questioning attitude. First of all, it is possible that your child may *not* have a genetic condition, even if someone has told you he has. Anecdotal evidence from parents suggests that children are sometimes wrongly diagnosed in this area.

'It's very common for doctors to change their diagnosis, even of genetic conditions, as medical knowledge increases', said one spokesperson at Contact a Family, the umbrella group for parents' support groups in this country (see Appendix 1: Useful organizations). 'We prefer to call it not misdiagnosis, but rediagnosis,' she added, diplomatically.

Second, even in those cases where a child clearly does have a genetic condition, no one can ever say with complete certainty how that child will develop. This is because there are many other factors operating. Environment and upbringing can dramatically affect – for better, or worse – any child's basic genetic make-up. If we give a child a loving and stimulating environment, if we encourage him on a daily basis to participate in little games and interactions, then we are helping neural pathways to form in his brain; and even though we may have to be endlessly patient, we will see benefits over time.

The child's own motivation is another powerful force; and we can help build a child's will to survive, thrive and develop by nurturing his or her confidence and enjoyment of life.

If your child has been diagnosed with a genetic condition, you may be thinking that his or her potential is limited because our genes are fixed. Or are they? The answer is that they are fixed – but only up to a point. Genes are often described as the blueprint of a person, but that's a somewhat dull and even misleading image. I prefer to think of them as a more creative thing altogether – and I suggest you do the same.

Imagine your child's genes as an art kit, given to him by you, his parent(s). In the kit, packed together with beautiful precision, there are colourful paints, crayons, fine lead pencils, broad brushes, and – very important, this – the finest of fine brushes for delicate corrections to the work in progress.

If you think in these more colourful terms, you begin to appreciate the amazing creative force that lies behind every human life, and it becomes easier to appreciate how our genetic make-up is amended in all sorts of subtle ways. When you let go of the fixed, immutable blueprint idea, you realize that your child has the potential to do better after all.

Some genetic and other diagnosed problems are degenerative in nature, and thus far we lack the ability to do much about this, although in many cases we may be able to slow down the process. But in the future, it's probable that more will be possible. So whatever your child's situation, you can always ensure that he or she has an optimum quality of life.

I once had breakfast with a man in his twenties who was shortly to die of a long-term condition. We were in his house, and I was struck by the good quality that lay all around us. The bread was better than the loaves I usually bought at that time. The orange juice was pressed, not concentrated. The spread was butter, not margarine.

I thought about the difference: this habitual breakfast probably cost just a few pence more than mine, but the quality was so much better. And then it struck me that we are all dying, though most of us have longer on this planet than my host that day. It made me realize that the little things of life are to be savoured, because that way we live each moment of our lives to the full.

This is something that parents of children with special needs do learn over time. Our lives may be more fraught, more uncertain, and sometimes more scary, but that's all the more reason to be open today to all the pleasures of being alive – and to bring up our children to feel the same. We can enjoy simple things like good breakfast foods, a walk in a park or by the sea, and we can *really* take it in, *really* appreciate it, because we do not take these things for granted in the way that many people without health problems do.

So if you're told that your child has a genetic condition, remember that your son or daughter still has the ability to enjoy life on his or her own terms, and that they still have unrealized potential. No one can ever say how that potential will shape up over time.

And, after all, we all have genetic conditions. My blue eyes and your brown hair are genetic conditions. Hopefully, we can accept ourselves just the way we are. But, if we do want to change these things, I can wear coloured contact lenses, and you can grab the hair dye. And even if we don't change our colouring in these ways, time might: eyes and hair can lighten or darken over the years.

This applies to all diagnosed long-term conditions, whether genetic or otherwise. In nature, things grow, evolve and change; nothing stays the same for ever. This means your child always has potential.

When the diagnosis is not obvious

For a great many children, there is no immediate diagnosis – and perhaps, after countless tests, there turns out never to be a satisfactory explanation. This can be harrowing in its own way. At least when you have a diagnosis, you feel you know what you're dealing with.

When there is no diagnosis, nothing is certain. You don't know how your child is going to develop, what future problems may become obvious, what his or her life expectancy might be.

Life expectancy is one of the things that obviously scares parents the most. One father wrote about it recently to an on-line support group: 'As we read all of your personal accounts, there is a terrible question that nags at us. A question that we don't know if we want the answer to. Where are the adults with my daughter's problems? Are there only children? What does that mean for us? I know you all understand the fear that we are facing.'

Not having a name for your child's condition can be very confusing, like having to fight an enemy you can't see. You know there is a problem, but there is nothing concrete to grapple with. Your thoughts can go round and round in circles, trying vainly to find an explanation that fits the facts. It's human nature to want to find a name to fit a problem. When you don't have a name, a diagnosis, you can feel tormented by the uncertainty.

One mother wrote about this recently: 'Sometimes I feel so guilty for feeling this way, angry, scared, afraid that I may have inadvertently caused his condition, sadness at all the things he may not be able to do. Is this normal?'

If there is a mystery about the origins of your child's problems, you may also find yourself wondering what caused it, what you did wrong. You may find yourself remembering something quite insignificant, like that time you drank too much in early pregnancy, or the occasion you ate unpasteurized cheese, or those weeks when you walked along a busy road, rich in car fumes . . . and you may believe in your own mind, for a while, that you've found the source of the problem.

But for every bad deed you imagine you've committed, you can be sure that there are many, many parents who did the same things, and far worse – and yet their children turned out to be perfectly healthy. Your child's condition is not your fault.

- *Fact*: Probably every parent of a child with special needs goes through a personal 'guilt trip', wondering what they did wrong.

- *Fact*: Thinking these destructive thoughts is a waste of time and energy – you need all the energy you can get for the task ahead.
- *Fact*: You are extremely unlikely to have caused your child's problems. Think of it differently: you gave your child life – and life always comes with its own lessons and challenges. Your child's difficulties may be more obvious than other people's, but we all have to face challenges – they show up sooner or later. That is part of what makes us human.
- *Fact*: You and your co-parent are the very best people to help your child achieve a fulfilling, optimal life.

When you start thinking in this more positive way, you realize that there is actually a great advantage in not having a diagnosis. It means no one can ever place limits on your child's future. His or her growth and development is uncharted territory. With the right interventions, including good nutrition, therapies and complementary medicine, much may be possible.

But if there is no clear diagnosis, you may still want to spend some time looking for one, and your child's doctors certainly will. This is when the testing season begins. Information on how to protect your child and yourself through hospital traumas is contained in Chapter 2. But first, here is a survival kit of general coping strategies for all parents of children with special needs: something to get you through the early months.

Coping strategies for the early months

Bond with your child

One father of a little girl with Down's syndrome says that as soon as she was born they were deluged with helpful literature, when they just wanted to sit with their baby, experience their love for her, and quietly get used to the reality of their situation.

I think it's really important to give yourself time for this. When you have a child with special needs, your world is suddenly full of a lot of other people who aren't necessarily invited: doctors, therapists, health visitors, maybe social services. You may well find, like many parents do, that you have several appointments a week.

All these people have views on the best way to progress. Their views can be extremely helpful, but too many opinions can – if you're not aware of the peril – get between you and your child. They can prevent you from getting to know the real little individual who is your child – and giving him or her the respect that every human deserves. This can have unfortunate effects on the bonding process between you and your son or daughter.

When you bond well with your child, it means that you notice and respond to all sorts of little things. You notice the subtle difference between an open-mouthed, desperate cry that means he's thirsty, and a frustrated cry that means he just tried to reach for a toy and his poor motor skills have yet again let him down. And you respond accordingly.

Or you notice that he's looking out of the window at a tree, and you say, 'Look at that tree, it's really moving in the wind, isn't it?' And by talking to him about what he's seeing, you have given him names for what he's seeing, so he's learnt a little bit more about the world.

When you notice all these little things, the communication between the two of you grows. You can feel the difference.

Here are specific ways to increase bonding:

Spend time with your child, just cuddling, enjoying, playing

Use a technique developed by two American doctors, called floor time, in which you let your child take the lead in play, and gently join in at his or her level. Imitate your child's movements, positioning and sounds, make little incursions into his or her activities, but don't get too heavy or serious about it. This is playtime, where the fun develops spontaneously.

You can read more about this technique in *The Child with Special Needs* by Stanley I. Greenspan and Serena Wieder (see Appendix 3: Further reading).

If your child has poor eye contact, play games to encourage him to look at you

Hide your face behind your hands, then part your fingers slightly and peer through. When your child looks at you, playfully hide again.

Look at your child through things that have holes in them – children with poor eye contact, like all children, find this intriguing. Try a kitchen sieve, a slatted chair, a wooden abacus. And move your face around so sometimes your child can see it clearly, sometimes he can't. Or put something silly on your face: a red nose, a cartoon mask, a dot of shaving foam between your eyes. Try anything, in a fun, lighthearted way that might encourage your child to look at you.

12

Don't stare too long at your child, or try to persuade him to look at you. If he suffers from poor contact, it is probably because he finds it too stimulating, so forcing him will just make him feel worse. You can achieve more by little fun, teasing steps like those above.

In fact, as a general rule, it's best not to force your child

If she refuses to eat or brush her teeth, don't force the spoon or toothbrush into her mouth. If physiotherapy exercises make her cry, don't force her through the moves. It may be tempting to try to force her, but in the long run it just doesn't work.

If someone forced you to eat or clean your teeth, day after day, you'd probably become angry and resistant. You'd feel powerless, resentful and out of control. You might feel alienated from the person who was forcing you against your will. And you'd probably be put off the activity for a long time to come.

In your child's case, it could be even worse than that. Children with special needs often have problems processing sensory information. Sometimes a part of their body may be hypersensitive to touch, or hyposensitive. If your child's mouth is particularly sensitive to touch, even the softest toothbrush could feel harsh and rough.

The secret is to use positive methods.

With teethbrushing, show her through your own example, or through her siblings' example. Get a fun toothbrush and a tasty toothpaste. Let her brush your teeth, pretend to brush her teddy's teeth. Sing a fun song. Give loads of praise to each tiny step forward. Remember it's more important to establish good teethbrushing habits for the long term than to get it right on day one.

With feeding, adapt the same fun methods. Eat the same meals as her, with her, and get the whole family to do the same. Eat a spoonful of her food and show great enjoyment. Take pleasure in offering appetizing-looking dishes. Let her join in with the choosing and preparation of meals as much as is feasible.

If necessary, take the pressure off and give her calorie-rich drinks such as milkshakes, banana shakes and special supplements such as Pediasure and Duocal which you can get on prescription – though if you come to rely on these methods, you may well find that she has even less appetite for solid foods. If she's a persistently poor eater, you'll find more ideas to help in Chapter 4.

With physiotherapy exercises, lots of crying can be a sign that she's neurologically nowhere near ready to do the suggested exercises. It could be worth starting with less ambitious movements, and also incorporating them naturally in play, rather than creating a set exercise time each day.

Give your child plenty of time for rest

Many children with developmental delays and other health problems actually do need more rest, because they're having to work much harder to make sense of the world.

There is a conventional wisdom that says, 'Stimulate, stimulate, stimulate'. This certainly is vitally important, but so is rest. If you feel there are just too many appointments, start rearranging them, cancelling or postponing where necessary. Decide in your own mind the maximum number of appointments that you and your child can take in a week, and never accept more than that figure.

And when she's resting, you can rest with her and cuddle. Which leads us to the next point:

Let your baby or young child sleep with you if this suits you

People seem to have strong opinions about this, one way or the other. But if it suits you, then do it. There is certainly evidence to show that pre-term babies benefit from being carried on a parent's chest; there's other evidence that suggests that cot deaths are less common in cultures where the babies sleep in their parents' bed; and common sense tells us that cuddles are healing – and that goes for older children too. Obviously you have to take basic precautions: make sure your child is not overheated, and don't do it if either partner has been drinking, or is under the influence of any drugs.

Sing, dance and play music with your children

Babies and very young children love music, and this seems to be particularly true of children with special needs.

As I mentioned earlier when discussing teethbrushing, many children with special needs have sensory processing problems: they find it difficult to 'read' the sensory signals they get from the world, so life can be a confusing cacophony of mixed sensations.

Music can create rhythmic order in the midst of this confusion – it can be very healing. So sing to your child – it doesn't matter how awful your voice is, your child will appreciate it anyway.

Play music too, as much as you can, as long as your child enjoys this. Classical music is particularly good. Regular doses of dance music can also be great. You don't have to spend a fortune on music – just turn the radio on.

If your child has a problem sleeping, classical music quietly in the room can sometimes help. If he hates getting dressed, sing songs such as the Hokey Cokey while you're putting his hands into sleeves and his feet into trouser legs; make up lyrics to suit your actions.

Discover your child's sensory world

As I've been saying in the paragraphs above, children with special needs often have problems processing the sensory information they receive about the world. This is absolutely key to their problems, and key to our solutions.

In the UK, doctors don't currently seem to talk much about sensory processing; in some parts of the world, notably the USA, doctors are more aware of this fundamental aspect of child development.

The standard development tests in the UK totally ignore sensory considerations. They look at your child in a very simplistic way: if your child turns his head in the direction of sound, for example, he can hear. If he doesn't, he can't. If he fails this test several times, grommets are sometimes suggested – that is, little tubes inserted through the ear drum, to clear fluid from the middle ear.

But hearing isn't just a matter of letting the sound in. The brain has to do quite a lot of work to process the sound, interpret it correctly, then give the signal for the eyes to move in the direction of the sound. In children with delays, the neural pathways required for some of this intricate process may not yet have formed.

Then again, maybe the child just didn't feel like turning to face the sound. In either case, installing grommets isn't going to make much difference. It's just another unnecessary intervention.

Sensory processing problems are extremely common in children with special needs, so it's worth trying to work out for yourself any problems your child may have in this area.

Simply being able to 'read' your child in this way can feel quite empowering, because you begin to get a sense of understanding his actions – and you stop taking his behaviour so personally.

If you notice that your child is physically sensitive to touch, for example, then you suddenly understand why she draws away from hugs. On further observation, you may notice that firm pressure is OK, so you might give her bear hugs. If she's sensitive to sound, you may discover that she comes up to you more often if you only speak very quietly and softly to her.

Here are some things to watch out for:

15

- Does your child enjoy repetitive movements, like opening and closing doors, or swinging or rocking, or does he like certain things to be the same every day?

  A liking for repetition and sameness are classic coping mechanisms for children who have difficulty in understanding sensory signals. For them, the world remains a confusing place, and the only reassurance they get is from little islands of unchanging order, or little patterns of order they can create themselves through repetitive movements. Children with autism and other pervasive developmental disorders fall into this kind of category – as may any child with delays of any sort.

- Is your child sensitive to particular sounds, like the roar of a plane, or a vacuum cleaner being turned on? Some children, including those classified as autistic, are hypersensitive to sound. One mother of an autistic child reported that her daughter could hear her parents talking in a room some distance away, even through a couple of closed doors.

- Is he unresponsive to heat and cold – can he put his hands on the cooker and not realize that it is hot, for example?

- Is she hypersensitive to textures: can she not bear to touch cold, wet surfaces, or does she hate going barefoot into a sandpit, for example?

- Does he have a poor sense of balance? Many children with special needs can walk, but frequently fall, or bump into things, or are generally clumsy. Some children feel uncomfortable with movement, while others crave it.

In all these cases, the children may have a poor sense of body awareness. Our vestibular system, the receptors of which are located in the inner ear, normally tell us where we are in relation to the ground, and whether we are moving or standing still. If that is not working perfectly, balance and movement are affected.

Additionally, there are receptors in the muscles, joints, ligaments and connective tissue throughout the body that tell us where our own body is in space. These together form the proprioceptive sense. If this is not working perfectly, we have a poor sense of where every part of our body is at any particular time.

Simply tuning into our children's sensory world can make a big difference. If we can get a sense of how they perceive the world, we can make them more comfortable within it, and we can gently encourage the development of their sensory perception through helping them to experience through all their various senses.

You can, for example, encourage your child to play with toys and household items that have a range of textures, sounds, tastes and scents. You can take him to places that are rich in sensory stimulation, such as specialized sensory rooms, or perhaps a humid hothouse full of scented, colourful plants. You can give him massages, take him to the children's playground, take him swimming.

Go at his pace, and don't continue with anything he's unhappy about. In this as in all things, children progress faster through enjoyment and pleasure than through being forced into something they don't enjoy.

The good news is you don't have to do this all on your own: there are also some experts you can call on, though it helps to know what you're asking for.

In the UK, occupational therapists, speech therapists and physio-therapists are increasingly looking at sensory processing issues, and they do have therapies they can teach you to do at home involving techniques like skin brushing and physical movements like swinging, rolling and bouncing on big therapy balls, all of which can help. A lot of it comes under the label of 'sensory integration therapy', so ask them about that.

If you don't currently have access to any of these therapists but think your son or daughter could be helped by one or all of them, ask your GP to refer your child for each of these therapies and, if necessary, chase up at intervals by saying that it is urgent.

Complementary medicine, such as homeopathy, can also make a major difference over time, as I have found with my own son. You can find out more about this in Chapter 5.

Help yourself to cope

Here are some methods that will help you cope in the nightmare early months.

Keep a notebook

Next time you go shopping, find a notebook that you really like: a pleasing design on the cover, pages with rules the right width for you, or blank pages if you prefer. This is to be your own personal notebook, to be used as you wish. Here are some things you might like to use it for:

- Record your feelings – it's very therapeutic to write them down.
- Write down your dreams. During critical times like this, dreams are

often more vivid, and may contain ideas on how to cope with the particular dilemmas you face. You don't have to analyse your dreams endlessly: just write them down and think about them, and you may find that flashes of insight come to you.

When your dreams are miserable, constrictive and otherwise unpleasant, they can often be a signal that your own actions are not the best ones for the situation you face. Perhaps you're being fearful, defensive, or following a course of action that your inner self believes to be wrong. Your dreams might even show backward movement of some description, or arrested movement, such as a crashed car.

Try to change your approach to a more positive, hopeful, expansive one. Be bold, believe in the future; and if you find your dreams become more positive and happy, you can be sure you're moving in the right direction again.

- Draw or paint pictures. Again, this is therapeutic, and it doesn't matter if you don't consider yourself much of an artist – just buy yourself a packet of crayons, or a little box of watercolour paints (or borrow the children's), and let your creativity out!
- Record your child's small steps of progress.
- Write down inspiring quotes that you come across – quotes that help you to feel more positive.
- When you're feeling down, write down five things that you're grateful for – this is a simple way of lightening your mood.

You can use the same notebook (or, if you prefer, keep a separate book) for practical notes such as the following:

- Record relevant bits of research you've come across in books or on the internet, useful contact numbers and so on.
- Write down questions that you might want to ask at the next medical appointment. Take the notebook with you and write down any relevant notes on the spot.
- Keep a record of all your child's various experts, tests and treatments – both orthodox and complementary medicine.

Keep a 'teddy bear'

By this, I don't mean a real teddy bear, but some kind of regular treat that reminds you of who you are. The medical world we find ourselves immersed in is not, let's face it, known for its sense of style or aesthetics. It can be a dreary place, and it's also not particularly interested in your identity, other than as the parent of a child with special needs.

A 'teddy bear' can restore your sense of who you are, and bring you some much-needed pleasure. Here are some suggestions. Feel free to have more than one 'teddy bear'!

- A subscription to a favourite glossy magazine – one that will leave you feeling positive and optimistic. Whatever you like best is the key here: that might mean anything from *Vogue* to a motorboat magazine, depending on your interests.
- A small selection of favourite mail order catalogues: Next Direct, Racing Green, whatever you like. It's amazing how a quick browse through the Racing Green catalogue can give you a sense of style and pleasure during a dismal overnight stay in hospital.
- Take up a calming hobby that you can carry anywhere with you – including those overnight hospital stays. Tapestry or cross stitch are both good options.
- Invest in an eau de toilette that you love – this applies to men and women alike. A good scent can lift your spirits, and a bottle lasts for ages, so you can wear it every day, especially on the days you have medical appointments. Consider it a scented aura around yourself, extending your personal presence, protecting you from all those nasty negative vibes.
- Consider treating yourself to a crystal necklace, or a little bag of healing stones. Crystals have long been believed to have strengthening, energizing and healing powers. Choose whichever crystals appeal to you at the time, and be ready to change them as you move into new stages of coping.

   In the early days, I loved wearing a haematite stone, which is said to be strengthening in times of change. Nowadays, I tend to wear amethyst, rock quartz or lapis lazuli, all of which are said to be healing, and make me feel good.
- Dress fairly smartly, in a casual sort of way, for medical appointments. The right soft, comfortable clothes do help to make you feel better, your body language improves, and people respond to you accordingly.
- Find someone, or a few people, you can talk to about everything that's going on. Of course, hopefully, you'll be talking to your partner, but he or she is also going through what you're going through. Therefore it can help to have one or two understanding, supportive friends or relatives. Make sure you don't *only* offload on

to them, though. Remember to ask them about their day, and listen to their answers.

- Sometimes it's nice simply to go out and have fun. If you're a woman, go out for the occasional 'girlie night'; if you're a man, go out with the 'boys' (actually, I think men do more of this than women, so they might not need encouraging!).

Look after your own health

One father, during the first year in which his daughter had been diagnosed as 'special needs', developed high blood pressure, and he says that he's sure the stress of dealing with tests, and arguing with health professionals, had a lot to do with it.

He was arguing mainly about whether his daughter with pervasive development disorder should go to a special school, or to the local primary. He favoured the local primary, but he found arguing his case very stressful.

Here are some valuable ways in which you can look after your health:

- Eat healthily. If you can, try to eat five portions of fruit and vegetables a day.
- Go to bed an hour earlier than normal two or three times a week.
- Take some kind of regular exercise at least three times a week, even if it's just a walk. Swimming is soothing – for you and your child.
- Spend a few minutes every day just sitting alone, doing nothing. Focus on your breath going in and out, or on a pleasing mental image, such as a beautiful flower. Try to think of nothing except your breath, or the image. This is meditation at its simplest.
- Take up simple relaxation exercises – yoga, t'ai chi and qi gong are all ideal. If you can't get to classes, buy a book or a video to follow at home.
- Do not underestimate the power of the bath. The children are finally asleep. The bath is beckoning. Add scented oils, use candlelight, and then just relax in the warm water.

Develop a positive outlook

A positive outlook can make a great deal of difference to you, your child, and the whole family. An easy, effective way to improve your outlook is to use daily affirmations. These were invented by the French doctor Emile Coué, who coined the most famous affirmation of them all: 'Every day, in every way, I'm getting better and better.'

20

He suggested that his patients repeat this morning and evening, 15 to 20 times, and it's a good policy for us to adopt too. You could also say it on your child's behalf, simply by putting his or her name in place of 'I'm'. Try it right now: can you feel how much better it makes you feel?

Many people find it works well to repeat affirmations just three times, several times a day, whenever we feel like it. You can come up with several to suit the various challenges and negative thoughts in your life right now. This is an ideal antidote to the dismal utterances of many medical people, which can actually act on our minds as negative affirmations.

Here are a few suggestions you can use or adapt to suit yourself:

'I am a happy, confident, loving and effective parent.'
'My child has radiant good health.'
'Every day, my child is growing bigger and stronger.'
'I welcome this day and the gifts it will bring me.'

Find an expression that you're comfortable with to describe your child's condition.

People may ask you what's wrong with your child, and this can hurt. One father replies, 'Nothing, she's perfect', and smiles confidently. Another mother I know always answers 'Why?' in response to the question – which can lead to some useful conversations. Yet another says, 'He's having a sickly childhood.' Or you could try the non-committal answer that says everything and nothing: 'He's just a little boy on his way to the shops', smile serenely, and carry on.

I know parents who say things along the lines of 'Mind your own (insert swear word of choice!) business', and maybe, if provoked, I'll indulge in that answer myself one of these days.

If someone comments unfavourably on some aspect of your child's appearance – and it does happen – then you could look in astonishment at your child, as though you've never noticed the alleged impediment, turn to the enquirer and say, 'Don't you think he's gorgeous?' This is guaranteed to cover the enquirer in confusion.

But, as a general rule, defensive answers don't leave you feeling too good, whereas being open and friendly, and willing to talk, leaves you feeling happier and more OK about the world.

If someone says, 'I don't know how you cope', you can say, gently: 'I think perhaps we look at it differently.' Or else you could say, 'We're very proud of Emma.'

21

Remember, you can choose the language to suit you. If you don't like the term 'disabled' – and many of us don't – you don't have to use it. You can use the words 'health problems' instead.

You could decide on a simple, natural way of describing your child's condition. In my case, if I feel like giving any details I say, 'He's got low muscle tone.' And sometimes I add, 'But it's getting better.' People can understand this, it sounds pretty *normal* (albeit *unusual*), and it conveys the sense, which is true, that his muscle tone is gradually improving over time.

Instead of 'low muscle tone', I could use the medical term 'hypotonia', but I don't favour using obscure medical language in everyday situations. It's alienating to others, and it makes us stand out as different, which is just what we don't want to be.

As I mentioned earlier, most medical conditions are still couched in Latin or Greek – and talking in ancient classical languages is, let's face it, considered rather fusty behaviour. Can you imagine going into a bread shop, say, and asking for *panis*? You'd certainly come across as a little bit weird!

Even well-known conditions can sometimes sound better if you put them into plain English. Take epilepsy, which as some sufferers will tell you, still carries a slight social stigma – few people actually enjoy admitting to it.

If your child has epilepsy, also known as fits or seizures, you should feel free to experiment until you come up with language that you feel comfortable with. You could say your child has blackouts, or that he or she sometimes has blank spells, or absent moments, or you may come up with something else entirely that suits your purpose.

Basically, by changing the language you use for your child, you are adopting a sound public relations technique: you are changing the way (for the better) that other people will perceive your child. Of course, if you prefer to use the medical term, that's fine too – it's absolutely your choice. But the point is: you *do* have a choice.

It can also be helpful to add a positive statement to a negative one to give a more balanced picture of your child. For example: 'He has delays, but he's bright and he's getting there.' Or: 'She has problems with muscular co-ordination, but she's a whizz at the computer.'

It may feel odd to 'talk your child up' in this way, especially if you were brought up to downplay strengths. But being positive will have a beneficial effect on your child. After all, we all flourish best in an atmosphere of encouragement.

An added benefit of a thoughtful answer that is at least partially positive, is that the child himself will be reassured by the non-scary, upbeat language. And even if you think your child doesn't understand, the chances are that he or she does, at least a little bit.

Food for thought

- There is a difference between the primary problem and secondary problems.

- A primary problem is the actual health, behavioural, learning or developmental problem that your child happens to have.

- Secondary problems are the problems that may come about as a result of that primary problem. Sometimes, if you understand what's going on, secondary problems can be minimized or avoided altogether.

- Examples of secondary problems may include violence, self-biting, excessive crying or other signs of frustration. They may include rocking, swinging, head-banging and other repetitive habits that the child uses for comfort. They may include active avoidance of hugs, sandpits and noisy places because the child's sensory processing apparatus interprets these things as excessive.

- The more you can 'read' your child, the more you will understand his or her sensitivities. The more you understand them, the more appropriately you will respond, and the happier your child will be. And a happy child is likely to have fewer secondary problems.

2
Coping with the medical world

As soon as a problem is noticed, your child will be examined, referred to specialists for consultations and tests, and perhaps given treatment.

The upside of living in Britain is that we do have free access to a superb medical system, which takes particular care of children. The downside is that you don't know whether the doctor recommending a course of treatment is right or wrong. In the early days you may assume that the doctors are always right. Later, you may worry about a particular drug's side effects, and question its usage. However, as your shock subsides (and this can take many months), you will probably become more discriminating about the medical care on offer.

What medical care your child is offered varies according to where you live. Some parents have a real struggle to get anything – this applies especially to practical interventions, such as occupational therapy, physiotherapy and speech therapy, all of which really can make a big difference.

If you're in this situation, it becomes more important to have a diagnosis for your child, because the health services are trained to respond to a diagnosis. So getting a diagnosis often becomes the priority.

Whether you have a diagnosis or not, chasing up by phone or letter will probably become the next priority. Perhaps you've asked the GP or consultant to refer you to a therapist. If a few weeks go by and you hear nothing, you need to make a polite phone call to the doctor, or phone the department to which you've been referred direct. You need to be friendly but firm on the phone. You must emphasize that the case is urgent: that your child really needs this therapy in order to progress.

Chasing up in this way does make a difference. If you don't do it, you could linger for months or years on a waiting list – or even, one day, find out that your child's name was never put on the list in the first place.

Conversely, many parents find that medical tests and treatments are sometimes carried out when they're not strictly necessary. This is probably so that doctors feel they are doing something, and also because they are covering themselves from possible legal action from vengeful parents. Did you know that legal claims in obstetrics and gynaecology account for over two-thirds of all money spent by the NHS on litigation? Doctors are right to feel nervous.

You may want to make sure every conceivable test is done, and your child's doctors may feel the same. But all tests carry the possibility of side-effects or complications, and all such procedures can be traumatic for your child. For these reasons, you may start to become picky about tests, rejecting those that are not strictly necessary. Start asking why a particular test has been proposed, and consider each test on its own merits, rather than automatically following the consultant's directives.

On the other hand, if you feel your child is not getting all the tests and treatment that seem appropriate, ask for them. In Chapter 3, you'll find pointers on how to discover what treatment others in your child's position are receiving.

Remember one fundamental fact: a consultant is exactly that – someone with specific skills whom you are consulting. You don't have to follow all the advice if some of it seems inappropriate to your situation.

Step inside the mind of a doctor

A very useful technique right from the start is to step inside the mind of your child's doctor. Looking at life from a doctor's point of view can be surprising. For a start, doctors know they don't have all the answers – but they feel under pressure from parents to pretend that they do. That's one reason why GPs over-prescribe drugs, and why consultants order too many tests.

As a society we do put enormous responsibility on to our doctors. Look at almost any medicine or nutritional supplement that you can buy over the counter, and in the instructions there'll be a little cop-out clause that tells you to consult your doctor before taking it. We expect doctors to know everything, and when we discover that they've made mistakes – which they do, as they're only human – we are full of anger: doctors aren't supposed to make mistakes.

You only have to read the *British Medical Journal*, the voice of doctors in the UK, to see what pressure they're under. In issue 318: 1576, published on 12 July 1999, there were several articles devoted to this very subject.

One news article in this particular issue of the *British Medical Journal* reported on a recent British Medical Association senior medical staffs conference, at which representatives of the UK's 23,000 senior hospital doctors said that they were demoralized and disillusioned by an increasing workload. The chairman of the consultants committee said, 'The intensity of consultants' workload is unsustainable.'

Part of the reason why doctors' and consultants' workload is growing is, as I said earlier, that they are ordering more tests. But why are they doing this? In the same issue of the *British Medical Journal* there's an interesting survey that gives insights into what GPs really think about their patients. This helps to answer the question about tests that we have just posed.

A small sample of 30 doctors in south-east London were asked how they felt and how they responded when patients complained about them. The overwhelming majority of doctors felt shock, panic and indignation towards patients generally. They also felt anger, depression and doubts about their competence.

Many of the doctors reported acting more defensively in their work as a result of receiving complaints. Here's one telling quote from a doctor: 'It has changed my kind of practice from the best I could do for my patients to becoming much more defensive and referring more things for investigation or for consultant's opinion, quite knowingly inappropriately.'

An editorial leader in the same issue of this journal makes the point that doctors aren't very good at accepting failure, but they need to learn, because failure is a fact of life, and a wise doctor will learn from mistakes. It states: 'Doctors are being toppled from their pedestals. The old world of omniscience, perfection, and success is dead.'

Think about those words the next time a doctor tells you something about your child that your own instincts, as a parent, suggest is wrong.

The family doctor

Your first medical contact for a particular illness or problem is often your GP. Getting the right relationship with the right GP is vital. However, many parents find their child's GP is less than ideal.

In what ways are our doctors failing us? To find out, Action for Sick Children, a major UK healthcare charity, carried out an interesting survey called 'What Mothers Want From Their GPs'. These were some of the criticisms of doctors that were uncovered:

- Many GPs make mothers feel nervous and ill at ease.
- Mothers often feel that their opinions are being dismissed too lightly.

- Instructions given by GPs are often ambiguous.
- In emergencies, mothers were highly concerned that it is difficult to get their child seen immediately at home or at the surgery, and that night call-out doctors do not have access to the child's records.
- Receptionists frequently seem over-protective of the doctor, patronizing and nosy.
- GP hours and administrative systems do not match the needs of modern family life.

On the plus side, the survey found that most doctors respond sensitively and quickly to children with rare conditions, and health visitors are highly valued by the majority of mothers.

Here's a checklist to test whether your child's GP is measuring up:

- Does she talk to you as an equal, listen to your answers carefully, give you all the information you need, and say honestly when she doesn't know something?
- Can you see her at short notice, or talk to her on the phone at short notice?
- Does your gut feeling tell you that her diagnoses are right, or are you left with the uneasy feeling that she's diagnosed your child's illness incorrectly?
- Does she recommend courses of action that don't necessarily involve drugs? For example, does she recommend things such as relaxation exercises, a healthy diet or counselling, instead of automatically reaching for the prescription pad?
- Is she open-minded about complementary therapy and able to recommend or at least support you in your choices in this area?
- Is she able to act as an advocate for your child and speak up for him if you're facing a particularly pushy, or particularly lax, hospital consultant?
- Does she leave you feeling fairly positive about your child, rather than drained and negative?

If your GP satisfies all the above points, you have a good doctor. If she satisfies some of them, can you talk to her and explain exactly what you need? Being clear, in a diplomatic way, about what you want is the best way of getting it.

If your GP satisfies few or none of the above points, you and your child would probably benefit if you changed to a doctor more suited to your needs (if that's geographically possible for you).

Many of us hate changing GPs. We've been brought up to believe that 'doctors know best'. In that mindset, there is no room for admitting any doctor could be wrong, or at least unsuitable for our requirements.

'I put off changing doctors for at least six months,' admitted one mother. 'But when I finally plucked up the courage, it was easy. I didn't even need to explain why I was doing it. The health visitor, who worked at both surgeries, just said, "The doctor you are moving to is very good," and left it at that. I had the feeling that she understood and supported my decision.'

Dealing with hospital

Broadly speaking, you are likely to face day visits to hospital for consultations, tests and treatment. You may also face overnight or longer stays in hospital for all the above, and possibly for operations or for periods of actual illness. Sadly, many of our children are particularly vulnerable to pneumonia and other maladies.

My son has seen many specialists in a total of six hospitals, and we have stayed over at three of them. In all those places, I have met countless other children and their parents, in for a whole variety of reasons from monitoring to intensive surgery. So I have the dubious privilege of understanding something of what you may face – and I have collected effective coping strategies from myself and other parents.

Day appointments

Minimize the long wait

Waiting times can be very long, something which all parents hate. After one particularly dreadful day, I vowed never to wait longer than an hour ever again and, funnily enough, I haven't had to since – so far, at least.

If the waiting room looks crowded, ask the receptionist when you check in how long you are likely to wait. Having some idea does help – and it may even mean you have time to nip out for a short break. Here are some tips:

- Take survival rations. Juice and non-messy eats for your child; juice and a cereal bar for you. If you're breastfeeding, it's especially important to look after your own energy levels.

- Take tempting, tiny toys. Although most waiting rooms have a good supply of toys, you could get caught out.
- Remember the really obvious things like tissues, spare nappies or baby wipes.
- Take small change – for the car park, bus or vending machine.
- Play with your child. This may sound obvious, but when you're in a waiting room it can be tempting to do just that – wait. Using it as an opportunity to play games with your child means that she is happier and more relaxed, and so are you.

Minimize the trauma

Unfortunately, many children with special needs become sensitized to tests – they can absolutely dread them. Depending on how much your child understands, it's generally best to be honest, without making too big a thing of it. Here are some more tips with regard to this:

- Let him know in advance what's going to happen, and reinforce the positive points: you'll be with him; it's a useful step towards good health; there'll be lots of good toys there to play with; and nice friendly nurses. It's worth saying these things even if you don't think your child understands – at the very least, your tone of voice will be reassuring.
- If he is going to have a blood test, it's definitely worth having a local anaesthetic cream applied beforehand. This will be done at the hospital, or you could get the cream on prescription from your GP and apply it yourself before the appointment.
- Give him lots of praise and encouragement all through the day. It's amazing what a difference little treats can make too. Spoil him – he deserves it.
- If you have other children, you can take them too, to give moral support. Or you can leave them behind and concentrate on making this a time when your child with special needs has your whole attention.

I will ask you only once . . .

It's very helpful to have some idea of what you're going to be facing at the appointment. If you've been sent a letter, and it doesn't make things clear, ring up and ask. Then, on the day, turn up with a list of questions – either on paper, or just in your head. Here are some good basics:

- If the doctor is proposing a test:
  - Why – what is the test for?
  - What exactly will happen during the test?
  - What possible results might there be?
  - What would happen as a result of the test?
  - What would happen if we didn't have this test?
      And, if you're still unsure . . .
  - Would *you* give this test to your own child?
- Other questions that can be useful include:
  - What is your gut feeling about my child's diagnosis/treatment?
  - Have you carried out this kind of treatment before? With what results?
  - What are the side-effects?
  - What are the alternatives?

Protect yourself

It is extremely common for parents to return home after appointments feeling drained, negative and full of tears. This is uncomfortable for you, and it doesn't help your son or daughter at all. The stronger and more positive you can stay, the better it is for your child. So tactics to help you cope are essential. All the strategies mentioned in Chapter 1 are particularly useful at these times:

- For the fastest lift in your mood, use positive affirmations (see Chapter 1).
- Phone a friend or relative and have a good moan.
- Consider whether you've just been a victim of the 'nocebo effect' (a phrase used by Herbert Benson in his book *Timeless Healing* – see Appendix 3: Further reading). The 'nocebo effect' is the medical equivalent of a witchdoctor's curse: if someone whose authority you respect tells you lots of negative things about your child, you tend to believe them. Over time, it can become a 'self-fulfilling prophecy'.

  Ask yourself if the doctor was being overly negative. Did you feel the doctor saw your child's good points as you see them? Or was she focusing on his weaknesses and thus creating a distorted picture?
- To counteract the 'nocebo effect', make a quick list of your child's qualities. Include little things, like her cheeky smile, and big things, like the fact that she said 'my juice' for the first time yesterday.
- You've just had a battering – you both need time to recover. So curl up on the sofa with your child, with drinks, favourite treats to eat, books, gentle music, a favourite video. Cuddle, rest and recover.

- If any painful tests or treatment have been done that day, it can be helpful to re-enact the scene with dolls. Put bandages over a doll, talk about what you're doing, let your child join in as much as he can. Add lots of caring to the re-enactment, and hugs and praise for the doll and your child at the end.

Staying in hospital

If your child has to stay in hospital, it's either because a test needs to be done overnight, or because she's ill. If she's in for a test, ring up and make sure you know everything you need to know in advance. If it's for an illness, you probably won't have much time to prepare beforehand.

Strange though it may seem, the two occasions that my son had to be admitted to hospital with pneumonia were both quite positive experiences. The staff were warm and supportive, and I was more or less able to live at the hospital with him and share in the caring.

In some ways it was a bit of a rest cure: all he had to do was rest and recover, and all I had to do was cuddle, play and generally be with him. And his father was able to spend long periods at the hospital too. The experience is bound to be more stressful if you have other children, because you may not be able to spend so much time with your ill child.

However, I came home feeling there are benefits to hospital care, which nowadays I incorporate into home caring. The main thing is rest: people do get time to have a lot of rest in hospital. At home there are so many appointments to keep, so many reasons to be busy.

Nowadays, at the first sign of illness, I give my son 'hospital at home' treatment: to do this you ruthlessly cancel all appointments; and make sure your child has lots and lots of rest, much of it bed-based, with gentle play, stories and little treats to keep him happy and amused. And, of course, you go to your GP straight away if the symptoms warrant it.

The fact is, children with special needs often do need a lot more rest, and it's up to us to make sure they get it. Giving 'hospital at home' treatment can nip illnesses in the bud, making an actual trip to hospital less likely.

Here are strategies to cope with life in hospital:

- Bring in your child's favourite cuddly toys – they can seem like a vital link with home. And these toys can 'explore' the medical equipment, making it less frightening for your child.

- Be there for tests and treatment that your child might find upsetting. If you can't be there, try to make sure your partner or somebody else is. Generally, be there as much as you can. It makes a huge difference to your child.
- Feel happy with what you're wearing. A good rule of thumb is to dress somewhat like the professionals you'll be dealing with, or maybe just a little more casual. The fact is, you *are* a professional in this setting: you are your child's main carer. And we all know how wearing the right clothes for the situation helps us to feel confident and at ease.

  It's useful to consider what colours you and your child are wearing too. The muted tones of most hospital wards and waiting rooms can be draining when you're immersed in them for any length of time. They can sap your energy. Bright, warm-coloured clothes can help to counteract this effect.
- Make sure you're comfortable about any tests and treatment your child is getting. If you're unsure about anything, request more information, or ask for time while you consult with your partner, and then together make up your minds. If you're unhappy about any aspects of treatment, ask about the alternatives.
- Make sure you have supplies of the basic drinks and foods that your child and you like: your child's favourite blackcurrant cordial may not be available in the ward kitchen, and your herbal teabags certainly won't be.
- Aromatherapy oils can create a pleasant atmosphere and aid healing too. You can just put a drop or two on a tissue on a nearby radiator, or somewhere close to your child's bed (but safely out of reach). It may be worth getting an aromatherapy book for guidelines. (You can learn more about aromatherapy, and the uses of specific oils, in Chapter 5.)
- Give your child massages. A daily foot massage is easy to do, your child will probably love it, and it will help you to feel closer to each other in an otherwise very clinical setting.

  You don't have to know about reflexology points: just rub the sole of each foot in turn firmly but gently – follow your instincts. You can use a simple natural oil such as sweet almond oil, and continue upwards over the upper foot, ankles and calves. If there are sore points, don't persist, but return to them gently and work on them over time. Only give your child massages if he is happy about it: the aim is for him to feel relaxed afterwards, because relaxation is healing.

- There are homeopathic remedies that can help deal with hospital trauma – both for your child and you. This is a subject worth finding out more about: from a practitioner or pharmacist, or from books. Two commonly used remedies are arnica for shocks and bruising, and the Bach Rescue Remedy to comfort and reassure at times of shock or trauma.
- Play music near your child. If you're in a separate room, this is easy. If you're in a bigger ward, you can still play a radio or cassette player very quietly close to your child – the sound needn't travel as far as the next bed. Play soothing classical music and children's songs.
- Make sure your child has plenty of opportunities for play. Make full use of the playroom, play therapists and all the toys available. If possible, get your child into the hospital garden for some fresh air every day.
- If you're breastfeeding, you may find yourself in the situation where your child is too poorly to breastfeed and needs a drip or a naso-gastric tube. If this happens, try not to worry too much about it. You can express your milk and feed it to your child by tube – ask the nurses for an expressing machine if they haven't already offered.

  Many mothers find expressing their milk very difficult – it just isn't the same as feeding your child directly. But even if you only manage small amounts, remember you're providing your baby with vital antibodies and other health-enhancing nutrients.

  If breastfeeding stops for days or weeks or maybe even months, you can still resume it afterwards. Ring a breastfeeding counsellor from the National Childbirth Trust or La Lèche League for help and advice if necessary (see Appendix 1: Useful organizations).
- Make use of the fantastic, free, highly qualified babysitting team that is looking after your child. Go out in the evenings with your partner. Make the most of this opportunity to spend time together, just the two of you.
- If you have to be at work, and it's your partner who can spend most time actually in hospital, know that your visits and phone calls are a lifeline for your partner, as well as your child.
- Let your other children spend a lot of time in the hospital with you. They will help your child with special needs to feel normal. Give them lots of praise for their support. Help them to feel part of the team, and that they are making a difference.
- Call on other relatives and friends to give help when you need it. Encourage lots of friends and relatives to visit your child.

- Say 'thank you'; give a thank you card and small present – such as chocolates, or a big basket of tiny toiletries – to the ward staff afterwards. They deserve it, and you'll feel better for having done it.

Therapy

The vast majority of children with special needs are likely to receive and benefit from therapy. Therapy generally takes the form of occupational therapy, physiotherapy and speech therapy. But there are additional types of help that come into this category. The most notable one is portage (see p. 35).

Probably you have great ideas about how your child can progress. Or, maybe, you're completely stumped. In either case, the therapist is, ideally, a helpful, enthusiastic, informed person with some ideas that are spot-on – ideas that you haven't necessarily thought of. She's a useful member of the team. She doesn't replace you; she helps you.

Here's a quick summary of the therapies. In practice, you may find that the different therapies overlap somewhat in the work they do, and the therapists will probably collaborate to some extent to provide a good all-over programme for your child.

Occupational therapy

This is traditionally concerned with helping people to carry out everyday tasks, such as getting dressed, using utensils to eat, taking a bath, and so on. The OT, as they're often called, may help your child to feed himself or herself by suggesting, or providing, specialist utensils and/or suggesting small self-feeding steps. They might help a child to learn the first stages of buttoning clothes by encouraging them to 'post' little discs through narrow holes. OTs might also provide specialist seating for the table or bath.

Nowadays, OTs are increasingly taking on another role: treating sensory processing problems. This could take the form of teaching you a skin brushing treatment that you give to your child several times a day to help him overcome tactile sensitivities. Or they might encourage your child to have contact with lots of different objects that stimulate the senses: vibrating toys, knobbly fabrics, theraputty.

Physiotherapy

Physiotherapy is about working on and strengthening weaknesses in the physical body. This can be done broadly in two ways. First, by showing you particular exercises to carry out with your child. And second, by providing props to do some of the work for the child.

Exercises might include things like showing you how to tap your child's chest to clear excess phlegm. Or showing you how to encourage a low-muscled child to crawl by gently positioning her in a kneeling position and placing her hands on the floor.

Props might include things like standing frames, walking frames and custom-made braces for weak ankles. How much you use props depends on your child and you. Some parents take everything their physio offers, then stick it all in a cupboard, and feel guilty every time they think about it. Other parents use everything diligently. And many parents make it clear which props they find useful, and which ones they don't.

The good thing about props is that they can help your child to achieve more. The bad thing is that they're doing the work, so your child's own muscle tone is less likely to improve. You have to find a balanced approach that suits your child.

Speech therapy

Speech therapy is actually about a lot more than talking clearly. Speech is a complex business, and many children with neurological problems and associated delays do have trouble in becoming fluent. Speech therapy looks at all aspects of communication, including the simple social interactions that precede speech.

For example, your speech therapist might show you games that encourage your child to make better eye contact with you and other people. She might also encourage imitative games, in which you copy your child's sounds and initiate some of your own for your child to copy. Or games that encourage your child to clap hands, pat his head, and make other gestures on cue.

If a child is slow to talk, the speech therapist may suggest some hand signs to help him express basic needs. And she will also look at feeding issues. The process of learning to swallow liquids, then learning to chew and swallow solid food, is in some ways quite complex, and children with neurological problems may get stuck at an early stage. So the speech therapist looks at all this, and suggests ways to encourage a child to progress gently on to the next level.

Portage

Portage is a pre-school home visiting scheme to help your child develop through play. Portage is not available in every area, which is a shame, because it's a great scheme. The word 'portage' comes from the French verb 'to carry', and the basic idea is that pre-school children with significant delays are given extra help by a home visitor, also known as a portage worker.

When my son was first offered portage, I was vaguely insulted. 'I don't need to be shown how to play with my child,' I thought. I've heard this reaction from other parents since. But it isn't really like that. The way to look at portage, just like the three main therapies, is as useful extra help.

Typically, the portage worker might visit once a week. She may come armed, like Mary Poppins, with a capacious bag stuffed full of interesting toys. Some of these she leaves with you for as long as you want. The portage home visitor suggests play-related tasks for you to do with your child to improve specific skills. She may suggest that you do the same task – for example, putting balls into a hole – several times a day for a week. And she may come armed with charts that you are supposed to fill in.

We threw out our charts after one week because we found they took all the fun out of learning, and nowadays we don't really follow tasks – we simply incorporate all sorts of play opportunities into the normal daytime routine. Other parents may well enjoy the discipline of charts and specified tasks. Again, it's up to you. But however you approach it, the portage worker, like the other therapists, can be an enthusiastic and inspiring source of ideas.

Assessment tests

These are a feature of every child's life. From birth, children in this country are periodically checked for physical, cognitive and social development. The senses of sight and hearing are checked, though others often aren't. If a child shows problems in any area, they are re-checked and referred for specialist help.

That's the theory, and it works fine if your child consistently passes tests. But many of our children consistently fail, and that is no fun at all. When your child is in this situation, you may wonder whether there is much point to all this testing.

The plus side is that you can use tests positively to help you get the best therapy/early intervention for your child. The negative side is that many tests just don't seem to acknowledge our children's positive qualities. Many tests are quite clumsy in their approach. Can your child put one brick on top of another? If she can on the day, she's passed; if she can't, she's failed. Can your child hear? If he turns his head in the direction of sound, he can. If he doesn't turn his head, he can't. But we all know there are many more reasons why a child may fail these tests, not least the fact that he or she may be acutely uncomfortable in the test situation. For this reason, every test must be taken with a big pinch of salt.

Bear in mind the following:

1 The only thing a test can prove is whether a child can pass that particular test or not. Real life is a lot more complex than any test.
2 Approximations of your child's developmental age can be very misleading. He or she almost certainly has strengths that are not being tested. Qualities such as abstract thinking ability, imagination, sense of humour and sheer dogged determination may not be looked for, let alone picked up during assessment tests, but these are the abilities that enable a child to succeed in the long run.
3 Always remember that children bloom at different ages, and what seems a weakness right now could eventually turn out to be a strength. A sickly childhood or late development can sometimes be the first step towards a glittering career. Einstein didn't talk fluently until he was four. If he had talked earlier, would he have developed his amazing abstract thinking abilities? Probably not.

Keep faith in your child's own strengths, which will become clearer with time.

Statementing – what's it all about?

You'll probably be asked whether you have had your child 'statemented' long before it's actually necessary, which is around a year before your child goes to school. The word is an unfortunate choice, because it makes many parents feel that their child has been sectioned off from the rest of society. To be 'statemented' sounds like a stigma, one that lasts for life.

But a statement of educational needs, to give it its proper title, is just a way of legally ensuring that your child has all the help in school that he or she needs for as long as is necessary. A statement is reviewed annually, and if your child no longer needs extra help, he will no longer need a statement.

You'll find more detailed information on statementing in Chapter 6. But for now, bear in mind that the statement is your passport to some wonderful free expertise for your child and you are consulted throughout the process.

A final note

This chapter has looked at how we, as parents, cope in the medical and educational world; and a large part of this coping involves developing a good relationship with the various health professionals we meet. Personalities do come into this: we find it easy to get on with some people, harder to get on with others.

When you don't get on with an individual, it often means his or her approach to your child's problems is fundamentally different from your own. However, it's worth listening to your own instincts, because they are a true guide to what is good for your child. Be prepared to change a doctor or a therapist if you can't get along with them.

Among your child's team of health professionals you will probably find some with whom you get on well. Consider these your allies – not your confidantes, but certainly your allies. You can use these people as sounding boards for decisions you have to make. Over time, hopefully, the allies will increase and be in the majority.

It is best to be a diplomat in your dealings with all the health and educational professionals you have to deal with because they form a local network, and they will swap notes in meetings about your child's case. So never be rude about any one of them to another, however tempting that may be. Remember that each of them always has the best of intentions, even if you happen to think they're wrong. Always see and state the positive in people, always listen and think about what they have to say, but hold your ground.

If you're uncomfortable with something, say so. If you're not sure why, say so. If you feel you should hesitate before making a decision, do so. If you feel another opinion needs to be sought, seek it. If you want to ask parents in the same situation as you, ask them. Remember your feelings are valid. In fact, they're not just valid: they're your ultimate guide to the best care for your child.

As you become more confident in your coping skills, you will also become more assertive in your relationships with health professionals. They will naturally respect you more, and it will be easier to get the right treatment for your child.

3

You and your relationships

In any difficult situation, listening to our feelings makes an enormous difference – they are our guide to the best way forward. In learning how to cope with special needs, dealing with our emotions – and that includes the many emotions we feel in our relationships with other people – is a major part of the process we go through.

In life generally, we probably all know individuals who appear to have good health and few problems, but who seem to be permanently discontented and somewhat difficult to be with.

We may also know other people who seem to have serious problems, but who project a sense of peace and happiness that makes them nice to be around. They seem to have learned the art of getting on well with others, even through difficult times.

We can all become the second type of person, whatever our problems may be – if we choose to. It's not the hand of cards you're dealt, it's what you do with them that counts.

The first thing to acknowledge is that, whatever your situation, you do have the choice to feel OK about it. Feeling OK means being aware of the reality of your situation, recognizing the negative feelings you have as a result of it, expressing those feelings, acting on them as necessary . . . and then letting them go. When you can do this, it tends to improve your relationships with everyone, because you're more likely to 'own' your negative feelings and not simply take them out on others.

Feeling OK also means changing the way we regard other people. It means accepting that every child, including our own, is a normal child, with his or her own particular blend of strengths and weaknesses. Disabilities, learning difficulties and other health problems are simply one part of the whole picture. And the same applies to all adults: we each have our strengths and our weaknesses.

In fact, feeling OK means looking at everyone afresh, without 'pinning labels' on them and expecting them to conform absolutely to that label. Sometimes we have to let go of old assumptions. For example, we need to accept that medical experts have their weaknesses, and children with special needs have their strengths.

Above all, feeling OK means recognizing the real individual who is your child, respecting and loving him, just as he is. It means acknowledging that he has had to go through difficult, confusing, and perhaps painful experiences, and he is coping with all these things in the very best way he knows how. It means being proud of your child.

Your child will benefit enormously from this positive attitude, and so will you.

Your own feelings matter

Here are some suggestions to help you to come to terms with your own feelings:

- Talk about how you feel to those family members and friends who are able to listen and leave you feeling OK.
- Be aware that some people will have their own problems in dealing with your child's special needs. They may not be able to help you for that reason. In fact, *they* may need help from *you* in dealing with their own emotions.

  If you have the energy to help them by listening and being supportive, that's fine. If you don't, be aware of this. Aim towards being calm and neutral rather than getting into arguments with people who seem, to you, to be reacting badly. Conflict uses up valuable energy that you need for the task in hand.
- Write your feelings down – this can be immensely therapeutic. According to one study reported in the *Journal of the American Medical Association*, writing about stressful life events helped to reduce symptoms of asthma and rheumatoid arthritis in patients with these illnesses. Four months later, the effects of writing these feelings down were still evident in 'clinically meaningful' improvements in the patients' symptoms. If it works for them, it probably works for the rest of us too.

  Write anything you like: what's happened, how you feel, what you dreamt last night . . . just write, write, write. It's great therapy, and it's free!
- If you feel you'd benefit from it, consider asking your GP or special needs centre about counselling. Parents in our situation are often eligible for free or subsidized counselling.

  'It just made things seem a bit easier to deal with,' said one father who had 12 weekly sessions with a counsellor at his GP's surgery. 'It didn't really change the situation, but I felt as though I'd released some of the pressure. I felt calmer, a bit happier, and more able to make decisions.'
- Join a support group. There are all sorts of support groups, including

local groups, national groups that focus on a particular condition, and on-line discussion groups. You'll find more information on support groups in Chapter 4.

- Finally, take notice of the other things that make you who you are. Being a parent is perhaps the most important job any of us can do, but there are other aspects of our personalities that need airing and developing. Give yourself permission to explore these when the time is right.

You might want to pursue a particular hobby, or you might enjoy starting a new course of study, or going back to work. Or you might find fulfilment in helping others through some voluntary activity, such as helping to run a support group for other families in your situation, or raising money towards medical research into your child's condition.

There seems to be something very life-enhancing about helping others. I have come across parents who have run marathons, climbed mountains, or taken part in sponsored walks, swims and dances to raise money for children with health problems and I have met quite a number of parents who help to run support groups.

Every single one of them has an aura of positive energy about them. Not all the time, of course: we all have our bad days and we all enjoy a good moan. But overall, it seems that by helping others, we help ourselves.

Taking notice of other aspects of your identity also means looking after yourself. It means, for example, enjoying clothes shopping for yourself, not just for your child.

It means pampering yourself with treats and activities that suit you, whether that means a visit to a gallery, a spell of gardening, a swim, a massage or whatever. It means following a favourite maxim of mine: 'When the going gets tough, it's treats time.'

It means acknowledging that you are a person who matters, one who never stops developing, learning and enjoying life.

You and your partner

All change brings stress to a relationship. Becoming parents is stressful enough in itself, but becoming the parents of a child with special needs undeniably brings its own demanding problems. The upside – yes, there is an upside – is that coming through the crisis together can be very gelling, both for the two of you as a couple, and for the whole family.

However, your relationship with your partner can come under strain as each of you adjusts in your different ways. If there are cracks in your relationship, they can widen. One partner may spend hours researching a cure on the internet, while the other prefers to think there's nothing wrong at all. One partner may think a normal, 'rough and tumble' upbringing is the best solution, while the other prefers to cosset the vulnerable child. And at times you may well look at your partner and be critical of the way he or she is reacting.

'She used to spend hours talking on the phone to her sister, while I went to the pub after work and drank, probably too much,' said one father. This couple knew that things were getting better when they were able to start laughing at the next medical visitor's foibles. Laughter is a great barometer of how well you're coping. If you can laugh at all, you're coping. If you can laugh frequently, you're positively thriving.

You may well be lucky and generally agree with your partner on the best way to bring up your child with special needs – but no two parents agree all of the time. Acknowledging that you have different approaches and reaching a state where you feel comfortable with this is important. It can be helpful to think in terms of the two of you being a team: each of you has something to contribute, and the overall package is better and more balanced as a result.

If you happen to live separately from your child's other parent, much of the above can still apply. You are still co-parents, each with something to contribute. And if your current partner is a step-parent to your child, the same also applies.

The other really important thing to say is that you are, of course, not just co-parents. You are a couple. As such, you deserve to be able to spend time together, the way you did in those early, heady days without children.

Even if you can't get out as often as you might like, you can still – with some ingenuity and imagination – create a similar feeling by having special evenings at home together.

One couple, for example, puts aside one evening every week for a 'date at home'. During this 'date', they do everything they'd normally do when out on a normal date: have a nice meal by candlelight, maybe watch a film (from the local video shop), take a stroll (in the garden). Sometimes they get their meal delivered by a local restaurant, adding even more to the feel of being out on a date.

'People don't always understand the concept,' admitted the man. 'One week recently, I told my colleagues I had to rush home because I had a date with my wife. "Where are you going?" they asked. "Home, it's a date at home," I answered. They were a bit baffled, but I think they quite liked the idea.'

The main thing is to do things in ways that suit you as a couple. The only rules for a successful relationship are the ones that the two of you make up together. If your partner is working late all week, have a candlelit breakfast. If neither of you has time to shop for groceries, do it on the internet and get the supermarket to deliver to you. If one of you loves spirits and the other loves fruit juices, have a cocktail.

Here are some other suggestions for nurturing your relationship:

Talk about it

However bad things get in your relationship, keep a 'door open' between you. By this I mean keeping open the opportunity to talk. With the right kind of talking many problems can be solved. The right kind of talking means that each of you gives the other the opportunity to say what he or she feels. You take it in turns simply to listen to each other.

You listen with an open attitude, and you don't interrupt to talk about your day. You might ask the odd question to make sure you've grasped what they're saying, as in, 'So what you're saying is you felt that you were excluded when Becky was in hospital for the operation?' Or, 'I think I'm getting the message that you're uncomfortable in your job, and would like to change, but you're worried about earning less money. Is that right?'

When asking these questions, your tone is open. Basically, you want your partner to feel free to talk about what he or she really feels, without fear of you jumping in and reacting.

Stay in touch

Touch is the most fundamental of our senses. Below the level of words and arguments, touch can connect us with each other. Sometimes couples find that every time they open their mouths, an argument can quickly develop. A loving hug instead of words can instantly change the dynamics between two people.

One powerful form of touch is massage. A bottle of aromatherapy massage oil by the bed can make a huge difference to stressed-out partners. Just glide the palms of your hands and your fingers firmly and lovingly all over your partner's body. If he or she is not receptive to this idea, start with something less intimate: a foot massage, or a shoulder massage.

If there are any problems around the issue of sex, then touch can do a great deal to help. Kisses, hugs and massage – for their own sake, not as a preamble to sex – are all ways in which love and trust can be reaffirmed between partners. When loving intimacy is strengthened through these means, lovemaking benefits.

Spend time together

Going out regularly, just the two of you, is very good for any couple. You may be lucky and have family nearby, or friends or neighbours who can babysit. If not, you may be more worried than most parents about babysitting in general, because of your child's particular problems. But there are solutions.

In many areas, there are babysitters available who have special-needs training. You could ask your health visitor, social worker, GP, community paediatrician or local special needs centre, who will know what's available – ranging from evening babysitting, to overnight respite care. You may be able to get some care free, or you may have to pay for it just as you would with any other babysitter.

You may not want, or need, specialist care. Perhaps you're just a little nervous and would simply like to have a regular, reliable, unflappable babysitter. Solutions that other parents have come up with include the following:

- Ask your child's nursery (or any good local nursery) if any of the staff do babysitting – many do.
- Use a 'granny babysitter' agency. Some agencies employ older women with lots of experience.
- Ask a friend's nanny whom you know and trust.

Ask a prospective babysitter around for tea to get to know them, and to let your child get to know them. And, of course, only ever appoint someone you feel totally comfortable with.

If you need any extra help, get it

If things are bad between you as a couple and you just can't work out how to improve your relationship, consider going to counselling together. You could go to Relate, or perhaps to your GP, who may be able to refer you to a free or subsidized counsellor.

Some people are scared of, or sceptical of – or just plain against – the idea of counselling. 'It's like opening a can of worms,' said one father who refused to go with his wife. But what counselling really aims to do is to remove the tinted spectacles through which many of us view our relationships.

At the time of falling in love, many of us have quite romantic ideas about how relationships should be – we're wearing so-called rose-tinted glasses. When things turn out not to be that way, we may react and think that our relationship is full of imperfections – we swap our rose-tinted spectacles for grey-tinted ones.

In reality, most relationships are probably somewhere in the middle, and all couples have their problems. Recognizing and dealing with these problems is a major way in which couples grow closer over the years.

At its best, counselling can help you to identify the misconceptions and prejudices that you each bring unknowingly to your relationship from lessons learnt in early childhood about how men and women behave together.

It can help you to recognize and deal with negative feelings such as anger and jealousy that you may have difficulty acknowledging to yourself. It can help you to learn how to talk and listen to one another clearly and honestly. And it can help you devise practical strategies for improving day-to-day life together.

In situations where a couple is facing separation, counselling can help to make that process smoother and less painful for both people and their children, and it can help separating couples devise ways of being effective co-parents in the future. On the other hand, it sometimes results in couples realizing that they don't want to separate after all.

If one of you decides to go for counselling, but the other one refuses to go, it can still make a difference, because what counselling aims to do primarily is help individuals feel OK about themselves and their lives. From that basis, we become less needy in our relationships because we're not looking to someone else, our partner, to solve our problems. We just look upon him or her as a companion, lover and friend, a person with his or her own interests and personality.

When we reach that point, we truly appreciate each other for who we are, which is the very best kind of loving.

You don't have to have counselling to do some useful soul-searching. For individuals who feel they're at a crisis in their relationship, this is a useful question to ask: 'What was I tolerating in my life before this crisis?' The answer is often revealing.

Another useful question for any of us to address is this: 'What is the lie that I have grown up believing?' The answer might be something that your parents taught you, such as, 'No one ever listens to me so there's no point in saying anything', or 'Marriages don't last'. A lie is a negative statement of belief that acts as a little saboteur in your dealings with others. Once you recognize it, it loses its power.

The benefits of 'visualization'

Whether you're getting on well or badly, 'visualization' can be a very helpful way of increasing loving feelings between the two of you. (For more on visualization, and a specific exercise to use in this context, refer to Chapter 5.)

Helping siblings to cope

Siblings have their own pressures. The 'sickly' child may get more than his or her fair share of attention. Older children may agonize about how to act with their friends with regard to their brother's or sister's condition. Younger children may have huge difficulties understanding that their brother or sister is never going to grow up just like they are.

Some young children come to their own, false conclusions about the future – a form of wishful thinking. 'My five-year-old son has decided that when his three-year-old sister turns four, she won't be a baby any more. She won't wear nappies. She'll be able to walk and throw a ball,' says one mother with a sigh.

Children can also mind – dreadfully – about all the tests and trauma that their brother or sister has to endure. 'Why can't the doctors just accept that my sister is different to us?' wrote one boy in an internet support group. And they can also become very sensitive about the terms used to describe their sibling's condition.

Siblings are often highly supportive and do more than anyone to bring on a delayed child. Apart from the parent who stays at home, they are the ones who spend most time with the vulnerable child. And their responsibility may extend well into their adult years into a time when you are possibly no longer around.

But they're not always noble about the problems. Just like us, their parents, they often wish, fiercely, that their sibling was just like anyone else, and sometimes they distance themselves in an attempt to avoid the situation. One six-year-old girl regularly called her little brother, who has cerebral palsy and epilepsy, 'stupid'.

On the other hand, some siblings seem to cope with total ease – it's just not an issue. 'I don't think my daughter has ever referred to my son's face as being different,' says Steve Moody, whose nine-year-old son Michael has a cranio-facial condition. 'To her it's just normal. Perhaps it helps that we've always included her alongside her brother in discussions about operations and so on. If you don't include the siblings, you shut them out. You create a barrier.'

Other ways to help siblings to cope include the following:

- Be a good listener to your children, so that they're in the habit of talking to you about anything that's on their mind. Give them the time and space to express their concerns and feelings, without jumping in and reacting. Make it clear that strong feelings are natural and acceptable in any relationship. Talk over the difficult issues that they face – like being teased by friends – and come up with solutions, such as ways to explain a brother's or sister's health problems to others in a way that feels OK.
- Give each sibling one-to-one time with you. You could create a special time on a daily or weekly basis. Ask them when they would best like this one-to-one time with you. Perhaps you could spend 30 minutes with a child three times a week, helping him or her to read. Perhaps you could take another child once a week to a football match.
- Give siblings time together with you. It's easy to let siblings just get on and play together while we get on with grown-up things. But all children blossom with attention. Make a point of regularly playing with them together.

  Do projects together. Here are a few ideas that children of all ages and abilities can enjoy with you:

  – *Miniature gardens.* Each child makes a miniature garden out of a seed tray and compost: add tiny plants, grass seed, little people and animals, a mirror for a pond, lollipop stick fences . . . along the way they'll learn lots about creativity, plants, and much more.
  – *Help them to make little books.* Fold and staple several sheets of paper together, then give them stickers and crayons, and get them to make up a story. You could encourage them to write/draw about specific experiences related to special needs – this is highly therapeutic.
  – *Let them act out hospital visits and other events through dolls.* Children naturally do this, but it's good to give them encouragement in case they feel they shouldn't talk about it.
  – *Show them how to make rainbows.* Place a glass of water against a window pane at a point where the sun is shining through. On a

table top or on the floor, place a sheet of white paper in a line with the glass and the sun. You will see a perfect rainbow.

You can teach them how to remember the colours: 'Richard of York gained battle in vain' = red, orange, yellow, green, blue, indigo, violet. And you can teach them a little lesson in positive thinking. In nature, we have to put up with rain in order to see rainbows. In life, we may have to go through hard times, but when the sun shines, we can make rainbows.

- Some families have weekly family conferences, in which everyone has a chance to speak about anything they like, and everyone is consulted on family decisions, etc.
- Give childen praise for the real support they give to their siblings with health problems. Your encouragement can help sibling friendships to grow stronger.
- Some national support groups run penpal clubs – a good opportunity for siblings to exchange views and to realize that they're not alone. Even if your support group doesn't run a club as such, it may well be happy to put your child in touch with another child. You can also make a point of meeting up with other families through a support group.

Helping grandparents and other relatives to cope

Grandparents have their own grieving to do. Like you, they were looking forward to a healthy, perfect child. But now, like you, they have to come to terms with a different reality, and it is possible that they may respond to you badly along the way.

Many grandparents are brilliant from the start, but others can be difficult in all sorts of unexpected ways. 'Just when I needed support, she seemed to be criticizing me at every turn,' commented one woman about her mother-in-law. Another woman became upset when her parents stopped ringing so often, and didn't mention the problem when they did. 'It's as if they want to pretend it isn't happening,' she explained.

It has also been known for grandparents to suggest that a newborn child with serious health problems be put up for adoption – a suggestion guaranteed to upset most parents dreadfully.

When grandparents are difficult, it is probably because they are full of fear. Generally, they dote on their grandchild and want to make things better, but because they're one step removed, they may feel powerless.

Generation differences also come into play. The way we bring up children today is very different from 30 years ago. Sometimes a grandparent may feel the old ways are best. 'She kept hinting that my breastfeeding wasn't giving enough nourishment,' said one mother. 'She seemed to think a bottle with a rusk crumbled into it would solve everything.'

Here are some things that can help:

- Talk to your child's grandparents: explain what your child's problem is in clear, simple terms. Don't leave them guessing – not knowing can be more worrying for them because their imagination will take over. Be realistic, but upbeat where feasible. If they are flailing around, unsure how best to react, they could well take their cue from you.
- If possible, get a leaflet or newsletter on your child's condition from a support group, and leave it with the grandparents so they have time to read, digest and begin to understand. You have to make sure you're happy with the tone of anything you give them – there is some depressing literature around, as well as lots of upbeat yet realistic reading material.
- Try not to be provoked when they come out with statements and suggestions that upset you – but don't go along with things you don't agree with simply for the sake of keeping the peace. You can hold your ground without feeling you have to justify your actions.
- Generally, be realistic but positive, and encourage the bond between grandparents and grandchildren in a gentle, unforced way whenever you can.
- If you're going through a bad phase, remember that it won't last for ever. Grandparents get used to the situation over time, and most do become very supportive.

Finally, on the subject of grandparents, it should be said that they sometimes find it hard to help because of the emotional barriers we, their children, put up. Maybe we don't want to talk, maybe we can't talk without crying or getting into an argument. Maybe we don't want to upset our parents and are trying to protect them from the reality of the situation by not mentioning it.

In the face of our silence, some grandparents worry that we may be refusing to face up to the situation and deal with it. They may also fear that the situation is actually worse than it is, because we haven't filled them in properly.

Sometimes you find grandparents joining support groups in order to find out more, help themselves cope, and perhaps feed information to us. And of course grandparents everywhere worry a great deal about the pain that we, their children, are going through.

To sum up, grandparents and parents can get on better by stepping inside each other's minds, looking at the situation from the other person's point of view, and empathizing rather than trying to make the other person behave in the way they think they should. Talking honestly, and being there to listen without judgement or unsolicited advice, are both invaluable.

Coping with friends

Often, mothers of children with special needs can't bear to go to mother and baby or toddler groups, and so quietly drop out. 'I used to go home and cry and wonder why she stuck out like a sore thumb,' said one. But it's important to lead as normal a life as possible. Stick with it and it probably will get easier. Or find another group in which you do feel comfortable and at ease.

My own experience of this is very positive. To this day, I still meet up every week with a group of mothers I met through ante-natal classes. There was a period, during my son's first summer, when I didn't meet them so often. I didn't know how to cope with the fact that their children were progressing while mine wasn't.

But they'd soon be on the phone, having a natter, staying in touch, and I managed to get through that bad time. I liked the fact that we did talk about my son's problems – it wasn't a taboo subject – but we also talked about a lot of other things too: from something funny one of our children might have done, to other medical situations that others might be facing.

In other words, my son and I were treated as a part of normal life, and that made all the difference. I'm hugely grateful to my friends for helping me through that difficult period. The sense of feeling 'normal' has continued ever since, and colours my whole approach to the subject of special needs. Special needs are not an alternative lifestyle; they are part of normal life.

One important thing you can do to increase your feeling of ease with friends is to feel at ease with the subject yourself. That includes finding a way of talking about your child's condition in a way that suits you, as discussed in Chapter 1.

It also includes not feeling that you always have to mention your child's condition – it is, after all, just one part of your child's rich and varied life. People will tend to follow your lead. If you can be happy, comfortable and confident around your child, they will be too.

Steve Moody, quoted earlier in this chapter, believes that socializing in the early years is also a vital preparation for school. 'We took Michael to lots of social groups,' he says. 'We wanted him to be familiar to other children, because people who don't know him do stare, and he does mind. But leading a busy social life in the early years meant that when he started school, he had many friends starting at the same time. And that made things much easier for him. It's important to mix. Although it may be tempting to hide away, in the long run it doesn't help at all.'

One additional note about socializing. If your child tires easily, or finds it hard to deal with too much social stimulation, there is obviously no point in forcing her into situations that make her uncomfortable.

But there are things you can do to help her enjoy herself in social situations. Sensory issues, as discussed in Chapter 1, are often key to this. Look at your child carefully in a social situation, and pick up the clues.

Perhaps your child is happier in small groups. Perhaps she finds acoustics hard to filter out, and so places with lots of echoes, like houses or halls with bare floorboards, are best avoided in preference to carpeted places. Perhaps, if she's a baby, she doesn't like to be handled by too many adults at a time. Perhaps she can cope with a few social gatherings, as long as she gets lots of rest in between.

You can build your child's confidence in social situations by ensuring that she's comfortable with the ones that she experiences. And aim to be happy and comfortable yourself, too. If you're anxious or miserable, even if you try to hide it, your child will pick up the vibes and react accordingly.

Coping with strangers

A common problem, especially if your child looks 'different', or behaves 'differently', is feeling unable to cope happily in the world at large. It can be immensely daunting to take a child with obvious health problems out on even a simple shopping trip.

Your own mood can make a difference too: some days you can step out into the world feeling happy and relaxed. Other days you might feel defensive, and expect the worst.

The only answer is to get out there and mix. Walk tall: you have a right to be proud of your child. Go with your partner, or a friend, if it helps. The more you do it, the easier it becomes. The more we all do it, the easier it becomes for all of us, as the world at large becomes used to seeing children in wheelchairs, or with oxygen cylinders, or with different mannerisms or behaviour, or an awkward gait or an unusual face.

In public places you may find strangers coming up to you with a smile and starting a conversation as though they already know you. Often, it is that they know a child, or children, with similar characteristics to those of your child. They may make assumptions that your child is like the child they know. They may turn out to be a health professional, or they may be a relative or friend of a child with health problems.

Sometimes, with these 'familiar' strangers, you may find yourself talking about special-needs issues when actually you just want to be a normal family on holiday. Remember you can choose what you say, and how much you say. If you don't feel like talking about your child, ask them about the one they know. That may well be what they want to talk about anyway. Or they may be looking to you for information that can help the child they know. (For ways to talk about your child's condition with ease, refer back to Chapter 1.)

One final point: people who know your child will like and accept him; they may even become protective and caring. When adults or children stare, point or make comments, it's usually because they're not 'connecting' with your child, though they are curious. We can't deal with all the passing stares we may get – it's probably best to continue on our way with serenity, if we can manage that. It helps if we can cultivate a relaxed attitude to this rather than a defensive stance.

But for longer encounters, you can turn a stranger's curiosity into a positive, caring force by helping them to 'connect' briefly with your child. It can be helpful to say something like, 'Would you like to say hello to my son? His name is Freddie and he loves it if you pat his hands', or whatever the case might be. If your child can talk, you can encourage the stranger to talk to him directly. (For ways to ensure your child gets on well with people, such as schoolfriends, when you're not around, refer to Chapter 6.)

Time for another child?

This is a scary issue for parents who have a child with special needs. The simple, inescapable question is this: 'What if the next child also has problems?'

The issue can have all sorts of unwelcome effects. It can certainly delay the arrival of the next child, though this isn't necessarily a bad thing: some children with special needs may well benefit from more one-to-one care in their early years.

The fear of having another child with problems can also put you off sex, put you off your partner, and fill you with an uncomfortable mixture of emotions, including sadness, anxiety, hope and fear. You may also feel inadequate, questioning whether you have it in you to give birth to a 'normal' child – and then you may feel guilty for not thinking of your child with special needs as 'normal'.

There may also be a feeling of dread at the prospect of possibly going through all those medical and school appointments with another child. You may feel you just don't have the energy.

And yet, on the upside, you may well want another child. If you haven't already done so, you may want to experience normal childhood development without the crushing anxiety. And the chances are always good that your next child will be fine. You may also feel, as many parents do, that another child will be extremely beneficial for your child with special needs. Siblings do make a big difference.

Contemplating parenthood all over again could well reawaken feelings of sadness and grief from the last time around. And whether you talk about your feelings or not, friends and relatives will probably ask you whether you're planning to have any more children, so you have to come up with an answer you feel comfortable with.

There is also the medical dimension to consider. 'If you decide to have more children, come back and talk to us about it,' said one geneticist to an undecided couple. What should be a simple, natural act between two people becomes a process written up in medical notes – in itself, this is guaranteed to put couples off.

Medical advice largely comes down to making informed guesses about the probability of problems occurring again. Many parents find this a useful first step in deciding whether to have another child. But the reality is that no one actually knows whether your next child will be OK or not. More often than not, the reasons why your child developed special needs will never be known for sure.

This uncertainty is horrible to deal with, and geneticists try to make things better by offering probabilities. Therefore you could be told that you have a 5 per cent chance of the same problem occurring, a 25 per cent chance, or whatever. But, as every parent knows, this still comes down to the same thing: either your next child will be fine, or your next child will have problems, and nobody knows for sure.

The arguments can go round and round in your head, until you no longer know what you think. One father described how he and his wife contemplated the options, including a donor egg, or donor sperm, or adoption. Every option made them feel sad. They wanted to feel OK about having another child naturally themselves.

Another couple got into a tangle thinking about tests during pregnancy. Then they asked themselves a crucial question. If tests found something wrong, and no treatment was available, would they take the only option, which was to abort? They realized they wouldn't – therefore there was little point in having all the tests on offer. They now think they probably will try for another child, but they're going at their own pace.

The best advice was given to another couple by a relative: 'You can't live on fear, you must have faith.' Your next child will be an individual, with his or her own blend of strengths and weaknesses. Whatever the weaknesses might be, you will cope, because that's what parents do. It's our job.

Parents who go on to have a child without problems report that seeing your new baby reach all milestones effortlessly can bring mixed feelings: on the one hand, you're relieved that the baby is all right; on the other, it rubs in the fact that the baby's older sibling may still not have reached these crucial milestones. One mother describes the pain of seeing her baby eat apple slices with ease, while the baby's older brother still has to have all his food puréed.

Parents who do go on to have another child with special needs often say it's easier the second time around, because they know what to do. They know the tests they want, and the ones they don't. They know how to get the sort of medical and educational help they want. They know which complementary therapies could make a difference.

If you are stuck in this dilemma – to have another child or not to have another child – one of the most helpful things you can do is talk to other parents in your situation. Again, the best source of such kindred spirits is through a support group; and through talking to others you will find that the majority of parents do take the leap – when they're ready.

4

Taking control

This chapter is about the turning point that occurs in every parent's life, and how to make the most of it. Sooner or later, the 'conveyor belt experience' of having a special-needs child – where you feel you're running to keep up with all the medical intervention and your own negative feelings – gradually disappears. You realize you *can* keep up. You have nearly reached the top of the learning curve. You have time and space to look around you, think about other things, find effective ways of coping.

With this realization comes valuable new energy, which you can apply to the task of helping your child.

It may happen for you in a single, crystallizing moment, as it did for me. One morning, when my son was 18 months old, I looked at him and suddenly saw the same little face I'd seen on my scan before he'd been born. Suddenly, I remembered the feeling I had before I knew there were any problems. I could feel again that he was my perfect, healthy little child. And all the depressing medical jargon about his condition just melted away, never to have the same power over me again.

Many parents realize more gradually that things are improving. One day you may look back over the past months or year, and register how much better you're coping now compared with then. And you remember how much time you used to spend in trying to make sense of your situation.

In the early months we all use up a lot of time and energy asking questions that are impossible to answer, such as, 'Why me, why us?' These questions feel as though you're hitting your head against a brick wall. You ask the questions, but you never seem to get an answer that makes any sense.

But gradually, over the months, something has been happening. Unless we become stuck (more of which below), we have been slowly shifting our view of reality, to a new view that is actually much more realistic.

We have been learning to let go of old assumptions about how the world is supposed to be, and instead we're allowing ourselves to see things as they really are. Every human being on this planet has challenges to encounter in his or her life. You could search the world for ever, and you would never find a family that has never experienced any adventure or grief – although many may try to pretend that they haven't.

When we can squarely look at, and accept, the problems in our own lives, we are doing something invaluable. We are no longer spending energy trying to pretend our problems are not there. Instead, we begin to channel our energy in its proper direction: into living our lives fully.

There is a big difference when we reach this point. Instead of resenting, enduring or being obsessed by the various things we have to do because of our child's problems – or else studiously ignoring them – we begin to see them in perspective. We let go of the flurry of negative thoughts that has been circling endlessly in our minds, making us withdrawn and introspective. Instead, we start looking outwards, at what is going on around us right now. We begin to live in, and enjoy, the present moment.

Even little things, like taking our child for a walk, become imbued with pleasure. We really notice and enjoy the small details, such as the haughty look of the neighbour's cat, or the exact shade of pink or gold and purple in the flowers that we pass. How much we can live in the moment, and really notice the world around us, is a very good barometer of coping.

When you're coping in this way, even the old, difficult questions such as 'Why me, why us?' suddenly do have a response. 'Why *not* us? Who better to cope?'

When you reach this position of greater strength, it's easier to make decisions about your child's healthcare. Whereas perhaps once you went along with whatever was on offer, now you're likely to feel in control, more able to make decisions that feel right to you.

This is a good time to review all the treatments your child is getting. Which are you happy with, which ones make you uneasy? Remember, as we've already discussed, consultants are just that – consultants. You can listen to them, and then make up your own mind. You are the expert on your child. What do you feel is lacking in your child's life, in your own life? Remind yourself, if you need reminding, that you can get it.

At this stage you will probably feel better able to organize practicalities, like juggling work and medical appointments, and fixing up childcare. And once you sort out the everyday basics, you can start to look a little ahead too.

Know your own mind

Many parents discover, over time, that healthcare decisions are seldom black and white. Is this operation really necessary for my daughter's happiness, or is she fine the way she is? Or is there another option that hasn't been suggested? Is this drug right for my son, or are the side-effects too alarming? Is there perhaps an alternative that will better suit him? When you look further and ask more questions, there are always more options available, one of which may better suit your child.

Whenever you face a decision about your child's healthcare, there is a very simple question to ask yourself. It is this: 'Does this decision I am contemplating leave me feeling more at ease . . . or more worried?'

It's useful to ask yourself this when considering a new course of testing or treatment, or choosing between a mainstream or special school, or thinking about a new piece of equipment. If you feel more at ease, you are likely to be making a good decision. You can probably see, in your mind's eye, a positive picture of your child in the future, benefiting from the choice you are contemplating.

If you're feeling tense and worried, it is likely that, at a deeper level, you are questioning the choice that you are contemplating. It is harder to project into the future and see a positive picture. Listen to your doubts. There is a reason for them.

Traps to watch out for

Sometimes our own ability to judge what's best is marred by other factors that can influence our ability to see a situation clearly. The best way to deal with these is to recognize them for what they are. As soon as we do this, they lose their power. Here are the major factors that can influence us adversely. Remember these, and you'll be able to spot them when they occur.

Beware of believing in myths

Sometimes we can feel relaxed and at ease for the wrong reasons – possibly because we are clinging on to an unrealistic hope. Perhaps, as once happened to my son, a consultant has held out the promise of a miracle cure. Of course, we all want to believe in miracle cures, and sometimes they do exist.

But when we're holding on to an unrealistic hope, we want to believe in a cure at the cost of the truth. To find out if you're being unrealistic, ask yourself if the facts really fit, or whether you are trying a bit too hard to make them fit.

In my son's case, the facts did not fit the diagnosis. The consultant believed Timmy had a rare deficiency of a vitamin called biotin. Biotin deficiency usually shows up in poor skin and sparse hair. But Timmy had very good skin, and his hair was no more sparse than many other blond babies. Yet in the hope of a miracle cure, we ignored these facts and agreed to the suggested treatment.

Unfortunately, the treatment upset his digestive system. On the consultant's urging, we continued with it anyway – we were obviously very keen for our miracle cure to work. Three weeks later the tests came back negative. Our son did not have the deficiency, so the treatment could not have helped him. But three weeks of an upset stomach left him with lowered immunity, and he then had a succession of illnesses culminating in pneumonia.

Timmy's illness may not have been entirely the fault of the misdiagnosis, but I was certainly left feeling that the so-called miracle cure did him more harm than good. I took it as a lesson: do not try to 'cure' your child at the expense of his health.

Internal preoccupations

Sometimes we can become stuck in a defensive mode that colours the way we view everything. When this happens, it has nothing to do with external circumstances. It is a reflection of our own internal state of mind; we have become stuck in a negative emotion.

The emotion might be a strong, obvious and extremely unpleasant one, such as anger, depression or hopelessness. Or the emotion might be a milder one, such as lack of confidence in our own or our child's abilities, or nervousness about the future. Even these milder emotions have the power to influence every decision we make. They tend to limit us, so that we choose the more timid option. These milder emotions may come and go in the space of a few hours, or last for months. On a bad day, lack of confidence can strike the most positive of us.

When we are stuck in a negative mindset, we find it hard to envisage a positive future of any description. When good opportunities come our way we view them with suspicion, certain that there must be a catch. This is miserable, uncomfortable, and not very helpful to the situation we face.

When we are stuck in a negative, defensive mode, we are likely to say things like 'Freddie will never walk', or 'Sarah will never be able to function without her drugs'. When someone suggests to us something that might help, our reflex response is to raise objections. Maybe we've lost the habit of thinking progress is possible, because the endless disappointments are just too much to bear. But, this way, we're programmed for failure, and our worst fears seem to have a habit of materializing.

For ways to feel OK about yourself and your situation, refer back to Chapter 3. Changing the status quo of an emotionally stuck mind can be hard, but the answer lies in the word 'change'. Incorporate any of the suggestions from Chapter 3 into your life today, and you will be introducing change to the mix.

To start the process off, say aloud to yourself, right now, 'I give myself permission to believe in a good life for myself, my child, and my whole family.'

Unhelpful experts

You can use the points that we've just looked at to judge whether or not you're happy with the various experts you encounter.

For example, you might realize that you're feeling defensive every time you talk to your child's consultant, or perhaps a particular therapist. When you meet her, you may find it hard to maintain eye contact with her. In between appointments, you may feel angry just thinking about her. You may even find that you're spending precious time and energy having imaginary arguments with her.

If any of this sounds familiar, take note: it's a signal that the two of you are not on the same wavelength, and you are not happy with the treatment your child is getting. Often you can improve the rapport between you by talking honestly and diplomatically, finding the common ground between you, and using it as a basis in your discussions. One area of common ground we hopefully always have with experts is the fact that we are on the same team. The goal of that team is to help our child to be happy, healthy and secure, and to develop to his or her full potential.

Sometimes, though, it's obvious that the gap between your viewpoints is too wide. In this case, a quick exit is often the best option.

Elaine Bennett, whose four-year-old daughter Maddie has delayed myelination, realized this forcibly the day she was given the results of her daughter's MRI scan: 'They gave us a wrong diagnosis. The consultant told us, "She won't walk, she won't talk, and she'll have no memory." And that was more or less it. "Next please!" ' Elaine continues: 'I was completely outraged. It was a terrible way to break news like that to parents. We were left reeling, with no support.'

The Bennetts changed hospitals shortly afterwards, and never saw that consultant again. Elaine used the outrage she felt to work more energetically to help her daughter – and with good results. 'I wish I could tell that consultant how wrong she was,' says Elaine. 'Maddie does walk. Hopefully she will talk. And she must have some memory, to learn how to walk, and do other things.'

Of course, it isn't only conventional medical practitioners who can leave you feeling uneasy and defensive. It's perfectly possible to meet unhelpful complementary practitioners too.

Usually the signs are obvious – perhaps she has a lack of qualifications or experience, or you spot some glaring inconsistencies or gaps in what she tells you. Perhaps she tries to tell you that her cure is the right one, and that everyone else is wrong.

These people are traditionally called 'quacks'. Two I have met were both totally unqualified. One proffered, unsolicited, an African tribal method of total healing that left me feeling distinctly nervous, and the other offered to sell me, for a vast sum (but it was, she assured me, on 'special offer'), a machine that would clear harmful electro-magnetic emanations from our house. The first imposed a vow of secrecy on me, the second suggested, darkly, that my son's life could depend on her machine.

Fleetingly I considered both their methods: when you have a child with special needs, the urge to seek a miracle cure can at times be almost overwhelming. But both these people left me feeling uneasy. Luckily I heard the warning bells and so, more forcibly, did my partner when I talked to him about these encounters.

Talking to someone else helps to crystallize what you feel. I realized that secrecy and scaremongering are not acceptable methods of helping a child, and that if something did not feel right, it almost certainly wasn't right.

Find your own path

When you begin to take control, you start to let go of the idea that an overworked consultant will infallibly come up with the right treatment after a brief examination of your child. If you feel doubt, ask for a second opinion. And if the second opinion sounds like an identikit version of the first, you might seek out other avenues, including complementary therapies and parent support groups, to find an answer that *does* feel right to you.

In practice, parents who are in control often use a blend of approaches in proportions that feel right for them. In other words, they find their own path.

For some parents, this may take the form of conductive education, in which a child is encouraged to crawl, walk, read and achieve other skills by a process of 'patterning'. You put the child's limbs through the motions many times a day, and over time the right neural pathways become established in his or her brain.

Such a programme is very intensive, lasting many hours every day. You may enlist volunteers to come into your home and do shifts, and that in itself can bring other pressures, as some volunteers may begin to feel more part of the family than you would wish, and offer advice in matters not related to your child's programme.

Conductive education is not always that intensive though. It can just be about gentle encouragement to enable children to do things for themselves. It's probably the sort of treatment you either love or hate. It seems to get results (sometimes excellent ones), but you have to be happy with what you're doing. Ideally, we're facilitators for our children. We're beside them, helping them to enjoy and explore the world, and thus learn. If conductive education is in tune with what you and your child want, then that's OK. But no programme should get in the way of real life.

There are other more specialized techniques such as auditory training, which is particularly effective in retraining a child's overly sensitive hearing. This has a good track record for children with autism, attention deficit disorder, and various learning delays. (For parents' accounts of this, I refer you to *Dancing in the Rain: Stories of Exceptional Progress by Parents of Children with Special Needs*, edited by Annabel Stehli (see Appendix 3: Further reading).)

An increasing number of families, like my own, are opting for complementary therapies alongside conventional ones.

In a way, my family's so-called 'miracle cure' experience was a blessing in disguise, because it taught us to be more discerning about conventional treatment, and reject things that felt wrong. It propelled us on to the path of looking for alternatives that work.

This has produced measurable benefits for my son. One consequence of Timmy's low muscle tone is that during his worst period of illness, he developed a spinal curvature. Two consultants told us he'd have to wear a back brace for 23 hours a day, until he had finished growing. After we'd recovered from the shock of hearing such a damning prognosis, we realized that the consultants' decision just didn't feel right to us. So we took advice from two osteopaths and a range of parents in a similar situation.

Then we made up our own minds: we opted for osteopathy, alongside occupational therapy and physiotherapy. One year later, Timmy's consultant examined the latest X-ray, which was clearly much better than she was expecting. Then she turned to me and said, in some astonishment, 'You were right, you made the right decision.'

Time for support and information

If you haven't done so already, now is a good time to make contact with other parents in your situation, through special-needs support groups. You can use them as much or as little as you like, and you'll never know how useful they can be unless you try them.

Support groups fall into three categories: on-line, national and local.

On-line groups

For on-line support groups, an excellent starting point is 'www.our-kids.org' (see Appendix 1: Useful organizations). Through them you can get access to a wide range of groups for specific conditions, as well as masses of more general information.

Groups for specific conditions usually work by circulating everyone's e-mails to all members. It's a great way to learn a lot very quickly about your child's condition, through the experiences of other parents in your situation. Feeding problems, weight gain, behavioural problems, toilet-training, mobility equipment, sleep problems, and the pros and cons of various drugs and complementary therapies, are just some of the subjects that regularly come up.

One advantage of on-line groups is that they're international, albeit with a strong American bias. This means that you get to hear what's going on in other countries, sometimes even before your child's doctors hear.

One disadvantage is that you don't see the other members face to face (though meetings are arranged from time to time). This means that when you post a message you don't necessarily get a response, and that can feel odd – like shouting into space. Many members don't post messages at all, partly for this reason. Instead, they lurk on the fringes, reading messages and learning from them. However, if you have a specific question that you want to ask other parents, you invariably do get some useful replies eventually.

Another point to consider is that on-line groups are not particularly confidential, though that doesn't necessarily matter if you take the view that you don't have anything to hide anyway. Naturally, you don't give personal details like your postal address out indiscriminately on the internet. Another inconvenience is that you might actually be swamped by too many messages to deal with.

Overall, though, the advantages easily outweigh these niggles. When parents first join on-line support groups, their initial messages often have an air of sadness and worry. Within a few days or weeks, the tone of their messages frequently changes to one of enthusiasm. Knowing that there are other parents like you, and that they are coping and that it's OK to vent your emotions sometimes, is a brilliant feeling.

National and local groups

The main source of information for national and local parents' support groups is Contact a Family (see Appendix 1: Useful organizations). This organization currently has around 500 national groups and 1,000 local groups on its register. All you have to do is ring its helpline and you'll be put in touch with a group relevant to you and your child.

If your child has a rare condition, there may be no specific national support group dedicated to it. The answer could be to start one up yourself. Contact a Family plays an active role in helping parents to do this.

Elaine Bennett decided to start her own support group for children with delayed myelination, with help and advice from Contact a Family. 'It's brought me into contact with other parents who have found good coping strategies,' she says. 'And it feels great to be doing something so positive to help my daughter Maddie, and other children in her situation.'

When Elaine told her consultant she was starting up a group, she found his response discouraging. 'He said, "It's not going to help you find a cure." I think people like him feel undermined when parents become proactive and find ways of helping their child,' she comments. 'But it's not just about finding a cure. It's about finding all sorts of little tricks and techniques that help your child to thrive. And it's about talking to others who understand, because they're in the same position as you.'

Local groups may concentrate on a particular condition, if there are enough parents in the area to form such a group. Or they may focus on a particular goal, such as inclusive education (see Chapter 5 for more on this). Most often, though, they may just be for anyone who has a child with any kind of special need, and who would like to meet and talk to others in a similar situation.

Local groups often operate under particular rules. One of these might be that everything members say to one another in meetings is confidential.

Another rule – which may sound odd, but can work really well – is to allocate time for each member to talk, while the others listen without interrupting. The group may divide into smaller groups of two or more people to do this, or take turns to speak in front of the whole group, or use both approaches in the same meeting. Saying something aloud to other people is very therapeutic. It's a good way of expressing and letting go of negative feelings, and afterwards you feel almost literally lighter, as though a burden has been lifted. This kind of therapeutic approach may be best done without children present – to give adults a chance to speak honestly.

A third rule, or perhaps it's just a good idea, is to introduce a different activity, such as a silly game, when things get too intense.

Other groups simply meet up socially, with their children.

If you feel a bit isolated, and could do with meeting more parents like yourself, a local group is a good starting point. Ring Contact a Family, and ask if there's one in your area. If there isn't, seriously consider starting one. It's not that difficult, and Contact a Family will give you all the help and advice you need.

If that at present seems too big a step, but you are conscious of the fact that you would like more social contact with others, simply state your wish aloud, right now. Say, 'I would like to find some like-minded mothers/fathers', or whatever the case might be. This may sound like a rather fanciful approach, but it makes practical sense. When we state our wishes clearly to ourselves in this way, they do have a knack of coming true. We open ourselves up to the opportunities that develop, and become more likely to follow them up. Go on, try it and see.

Time for happiness

As you feel more in control, and have more energy, it becomes easier to review the emotional atmosphere in your home and make improvements as necessary. Happiness and relaxation are conducive to healing. Stress and worry are not. So we want more of the former, and less of the latter.

Instead of pinning your hopes on some idealistic, vague time in the future when a cure may be found, concentrate on enjoying life here and now. Ironically, that's the best way to a happier, healthy future.

Stick this on your fridge door: 'Happiness leads to health'. It's worth stressing this, because for some reason we often decide it's the other way round. But healers have long recognized, and doctors increasingly agree, that emotional well-being leads to greater health, whereas emotional distress may manifest itself, in the long term, in physical disease.

Here is a quick check: today, has your child with special needs laughed? Has everyone in the family laughed, at least once? Laughter is good for us, and an excellent measure of our emotional health. Regular laughing makes us feel better and healthier, and improves our outlook on life. It helps us to cope with difficult situations, it helps us to see our problems in perspective. Here are some ways of encouraging happiness and laughter in your home:

- Watch comedy programmes and films on television. Video your favourites and watch them whenever you need a laugh. Hire funny films on video, or go to see them at the cinema.
- Tickle your child or children, as long as they're happy about this. Play those old classic games, like 'Round and round the garden' and 'This little piggy went to market'. They're good for teaching greater body awareness and anticipation – and they make children laugh.
- Remember the feeling you had as a child when you did simple childlike things, like crunching up the autumn leaves with your feet, or playing a favourite game. Recreate that carefree feeling with simple moments of pleasure with your family.
- Get into the habit of celebrating the little things. Buy a half-sized bottle of champagne and drink it because your child said 'yellow' today, or simply because it's Friday!
- Feed the senses. When arguments and other bad thoughts are circling in your mind, one of the quickest ways of improving your outlook is by choosing activities that please the senses. For example:
  - Get into the habit of listening to classical music, or whatever your favourite type of music is – just turn the radio on.
  - Place a couple of drops of geranium aromatherapy oil (good for the spirits) in a diffuser, or on a tissue on the radiator. (For more on aromatherapy, see Chapter 5.) Or plant a scented rose, or some jasmine or lavender, next to the kitchen door.

– Go for a walk and really drink in the colours that you see, visit an art gallery or shop, paint a picture of sunshine on water.
– Treat yourself to some new clothes, such as a soft, slinky, sensuous dressing gown.
– Cook your favourite meal, drink a glass of fine wine, or eat a tangerine or some other tempting fruit and really savour the taste.

• Do what you want to do, not what you think you should do. Give duty a day off, and just have fun.

Your child deserves to be happy

In a sense, this whole book is about ensuring that your child is happy, and you'll find a range of ideas in different formats in all the chapters. But here is a summary of helpful areas to consider:

• Cultivate an air of serenity, peace and calm in your daily life. Yes, I know this is sometimes a really tough one. But every child, whatever his or her problems, is very able to pick up vibes. If you are looking after your child's needs but seething inside, be assured that your child will spot it and feel bad.

It is not enough to go through the motions of caring; we need to *feel* full of love and caring too. So do whatever you need to reach that point: meditate daily, go to yoga classes, whatever. Try to approach your daily tasks in a meditative way: do them fully, living in the moment, and involve any children who are around. That's far more satisfying than rushing through everything but experiencing nothing properly.

• Aim for your child to learn through pleasure, not pain. Many children with special needs have to put up with uncomfortable exercises and other regimes, but some enlightened doctors and therapists realize that this is not the best way to motivate a child. Non-directed therapy is the name of this game: aim to spend a good chunk of time every day being a companion in play, not directing it, just facilitating it. Help your child to explore the world on his or her own terms, at his or her own pace.

• Shorten illness through laughter and play. This is something parents should be taught by health visitors, because it makes such a difference. Instead of simply gazing anxiously at your child, making frenzied appointments and worrying, aim for an air of calm caring and lots of rest, backed up with fun as soon as your child is well enough to cope with it.

Give your child favourite treats when she is ill, whether this is a Barney songs video, or a natter on the phone to a granny. Spend time talking and playing with your child. The sooner you can get her to smile and laugh, the sooner she will bounce back from her illness.

• Be proud of your child. Sometimes, when out and about, we can feel embarrassed by people staring at our children, or by some annoying habit our children have adopted that marks them out as 'different'. At these times, we are thinking negative, miserable thoughts that strip the pleasure out of any outing.

Recognize when you're doing this, and consciously think a positive thought instead. Say to yourself, 'I am proud of my child', and notice how different you feel.

Likewise, at home on a bad day, we can look at our child and notice the negative things, and let them loom large in our mind. When this happens, recognize it, and consciously notice the good things. When you do this, you can feel your mood lifting.

Empower your child

Give your child plenty of choices throughout the day: offer two or three options when it comes to dressing, snacks and drinks. If your child can't talk, maybe he can point to the jar of peanut butter or Marmite that you're holding up to show what he wants for breakfast that morning. Maybe he can just look at his preferred jar. Maybe he gives some other tiny signal that only you recognize.

Out on a walk, which way shall we go? Let the child choose once in a while. This is fun for you too, because being in control all the time is boring. Even a child who can't easily make choices is entitled to a life full of options and variety, at a level that he or she is comfortable with.

Think, too, about simple pleasures, like feeling good about how you look. Your child is entitled to feel the pleasure of different fabrics on his skin, or to wear the latest design in trainers and hear admiring comments. She's entitled to love the feel of a smart new haircut.

If we feel good when we're well turned out, you can be sure our children do too. And you can be equally sure that every child likes to fit in with his or her peers. Therefore we don't make our child look smarter than others. We let them wear their hair tousled if that's what all their friends do. If trousers are worn baggy this season, our child wears them that way too. If our child's friends are all insisting on the latest fashion, guaranteed to make their parents groan . . . we then need to grit our teeth and get similar groan-worthy clothes for our child!

One mother treats her daughter with quadriplegia exactly like her other children. That means if the other girls in the family are into purple nail varnish and Lycra tops, so is she. If they're into jeans and tee-shirts with witty slogans and trainers, so is she. This family lives in a hot climate. In colder climates, you have to bear in mind that a child who doesn't move much may need an extra jumper.

Many seasoned parents emphasize how important it is to treat your child with special needs like the normal child he or she is. 'If you treat them differently, they turn out differently,' says one mother. Even before her six-year-old son could walk, he was carried everywhere by his older brothers, joined in all their games, wore the same clothes, and today he's a happy, sociable boy at a mainstream school, consistently doing better than originally predicted.

Design matters

A sense of style can also extend to any equipment that your child's condition requires. If you feel that the rollator or walker provided by the physiotherapist is ugly and horrible, the chances are your child feels that too. Your child may have delays – but he's not daft. Believe me, however old or young, whatever his condition, he can tell when something is simply not 'cool'.

We all have to consider each piece of equipment very carefully: is it truly serving the purpose, or is it simply making a child feel bad among his peers? Is it helping a child to progress, or putting him more firmly into a disabled ghetto? Is it the right piece of equipment for him now, or is he simply not ready for it yet?

Sometimes we may hate a piece of equipment, and moan about how ugly it looks – but actually the main problem is that it's just not right for our child at the moment. When our child is ready to use it, we will look at it more positively.

Many parents moan about the poor standards of equipment – and with good reason. This is an area that certainly needs improving. Have you seen some of the monstrous, heavy walkers our children are given to use? Typically, they're big, and far too heavy, with quantities of dingy grey metal tubes and endless dirty Velcro straps that get constantly tangled up so it takes ages to unravel them. Specialist pushchairs and wheelchairs are not much better. We need to be choosy:

if an item isn't acceptable enough to be sold in Mothercare or Habitat, it's probably not good enough for our homes either.

If your child requires a piece of equipment, it's worth researching the options, because there is usually a wider choice than the small number of options offered by therapists. You can get company addresses and phone numbers from organizations such as the Disability Information Trust and the Disabled Living Foundation (see Appendix 1: Useful organizations). Trawl the internet, follow other parents' suggestions.

Consider whether something from the 'normal' world will do the job just as well. A trolley full of bricks or parents' shoes is much more fun to push than a rollator, and it provides learning opportunities for loading, unloading and transporting toys. You can get these trolleys in bigger sizes for older children.

Design or adapt something yourself if need be, or ask the design department at your local college to get their students working on the challenge. Students are not hidebound by what has gone before, and often they have a fresher sense of style than many established disability equipment manufacturers.

The best designs are often very simple. Take the Tripp Trapp chair made by the Norwegian company Stokke. It's made of wood, and fully adjustable, so the same chair can be used from early childhood to adulthood. It's designed to be good for the spine, and occupational therapists often provide them for children with poor muscle tone and/or spinal curvature. The Tripp Trapp requires no straps, and it looks great. And, best of all, it's not just for children with special needs – it's good for everyone. Whole schools use them in Japan, much of Europe and Canada.

We want every piece of equipment that our children use to be so good that others want to use it.

Food, yummy food

Many children with special needs have problems concerning eating. Dieticians can help with food ideas, and speech therapists can help with chewing and other eating skills. Speech and occupational therapists can help with sensory issues. Here are some ideas from other parents that may help:

- To build a child up nutritionally, dieticians recommend adding fats and oils to foods. This works well for many children, but not all.

Some children find it hard to digest a lot of fatty food, and may do better on a carbohydrate-rich diet. Aim for three even-sized meals a day, rather than trying to get so many calories into breakfast that your child is still full by lunchtime. Here are some of the things that parents sneak into meals for added calories and nutrients:

– safflower, corn or olive oil or butter or cream;
– peanut butter, or sesame seeds;
– for children with a sweet tooth, add honey, maple syrup, fruit or yoghurt to savoury dishes. Or dip a spoonful of savoury food into something sweet like yoghurt, fruit purée or even custard.

• For children with a poor appetite or low immunity, do what mothers have done for centuries: make good, nourishing soups. Home-made soups are rich in nutrients, and these are all in a form that is easy for delicate stomachs to digest.

Much of the goodness is contained in the stock used for the soup, which is actually very easy to make. For a vegetable stock, just throw a carrot, a stick of celery and an onion, all chopped in half, plus two cloves of garlic and a bouquet garni, into a big pan of water. Add other things as you wish: I often add three allspice berries, a mushroom or two, and sometimes a pinch of ginger. Partially cover, leave to simmer for an hour, then drain and discard the vegetables.

Some of these ingredients, such as onion, garlic and thyme (in the bouquet garni), have an honourable reputation in folk medicine for beating colds and other infections.

To make a soup, gently fry a finely chopped onion in butter for five minutes, add diced vegetables, then fry gently for a few more minutes. Cover with stock and simmer for 15 minutes or so until tender, then purée. Try potato, apple and carrot, or any of the winter squashes – onion squash is deliciously sweet. Or add red split lentils instead of vegetables. Or cook up potatoes, and add watercress towards the end of the cooking time.

You can also add flavour in the form of ginger, garlic, lemon juice or curry spices. Before serving, add a swirl of cream. You can follow a recipe book, or simply experiment. Soups and stocks freeze well.

• Never force a child to eat – it'll just put him off the whole process. Aim for enjoyment. If you find they work, use distracting methods for young children, such as a clockwork toy whizzing across the table; however, avoid making these a habit if you possibly can.

Singing while you spoonfeed works well too. Play an opera or a collection of children's songs, and join in the singing with gusto. Make up silly lyrics to fit in with what you're doing. Many children love this, and it can work well for other tasks they may not like, such as face washing and dressing.

- Let your child get messy; all children make a mess when they're learning how to feed themselves. Children with special needs can take much longer to learn, and we need to let them get messy for longer. Too much telling off and tidiness can be counter-productive. But, at the same time, our children may be more sensitive to sticky hands, so be ready to clean them up the moment they start feeling upset by the feel of food on their hands.

- Involve your child in the preparation of food, making it a pleasant, shared activity. From choosing ingredients in the supermarket, to helping to stir and spread the flapjack mix, to helping with the washing up . . . being involved in this way adds hugely to a child's enjoyment of mealtimes.

- If your child is ill or run down, or has been taking antibiotics, then supplements, including probiotics, can help to restore his appetite (see Chapter 5 for more on this).

- For older, more aware children who find it hard to eat and do other activities tidily – or even do them at all – get them a copy of *Leo the Late Bloomer*. This lovely American book features a young lion – a tiger in some editions – who can't eat, write or do anything much, unlike all his young friends in the jungle. Leo's dad is worried, but his mother just says, 'A watched bloomer never blooms.'

So Leo's parents let him be himself, and one day he blooms. He can eat neatly! He can write! And he can talk! This book has given encouragement to many weary parents as well as children. (There are many editions available through on-line bookstores such as amazon.co.uk.)

Food for thought

Have you heard of the Law of Concentrated Attention? It was discovered by the French physician Emile Coué, and it goes like this:

> Whenever attention is concentrated on an idea over and over again, it spontaneously tends to realize itself.

This is a useful law to apply to our own lives. If we focus on our child's illness, disabilities or learning difficulties, then we are creating more of the same. If, on the other hand, we focus on health, healing and normal life, then that's what we get more of.

What does this mean in practice? See less of the people – health professionals, friends, whoever they may be – who leave you feeling bad about your child; see more of the people who leave you feeling good.

And in your searches on the internet, avoid those websites with ugly words like 'disability' and 'syndrome'. Instead, look for positive pages relating to healing and health. Or, better still, turn the computer off and just go out and have a nice day with your children.

5

Complementary therapies

Many parents feel their children benefit from complementary therapies and treatment. This chapter is a guide to the most commonly used therapies, and how to choose the best one for your child.

You will also find ideas here on healing at home. Each of us has healing powers, which we can use to good effect on our children. You only have to think of how a hug or a compliment can make you feel good to realize the truth of this. Think about how, when children hurt themselves, they cheer up if we 'kiss it better'. Or how, when a child falls over, we instinctively place a hand over the hurt spot and that seems to ease the pain.

When someone doesn't use their healing power, you soon notice the difference. Imagine for a moment that you are feeling down, and you are telling a friend your worries. She reacts by looking worried and nervous, and tells you that you don't look well. How does her anxiety make you feel? Probably even worse than you did before.

And so it is with our children. If they are feeling poorly, and we react with worried faces and nervous gestures, they feel worse. If, on the other hand, we look at them with kind, reassuring faces, and if we speak to them soothingly and appear competent, and if we project a calm sense of love, then they feel better.

Medicine matters, but ultimately any doctor would acknowledge it is the patient who does the actual healing. So by creating a loving, positive, peaceful and caring atmosphere around your child, you create the best possible conditions for him or her to heal. And complementary therapies can be an invaluable help in this.

How to choose complementary therapy

Acupuncture, chiropractic, flower remedies, hands-on healing, homeopathy, kinesiology, osteopathy, reflexology . . . there are a bewildering number of therapies to choose from, but actually when you look at them closely, many of them perform a similar job.

Broadly speaking, complementary practitioners tend to treat the person as a whole, rather than treating specific symptoms. Such practitioners are more likely to see the link between emotions and disease (although conventional medicine is catching up in this respect).

73

Gentle medicine

This means that a homeopath, for example, might prescribe a remedy that addresses a personality trait, as well as the physical malady that brought the patient to them in the first place.

Homeopathy involves giving the patient a substance diluted so many times that the original substance is scarcely there – hence it is essentially harmless. This remedy, as it's called, creates the same effect on the body as the original illness. But because it's so diluted, the body can react against it and start fighting back. Effectively, the right homeopathic remedy 'kick-starts' the body into curing itself.

Bach flower remedies are prepared in a similar way but tend to focus primarily on treating emotions, on the basis that negative emotions are responsible for the creation of physical illness.

Of course, negative emotions are not necessarily bad in themselves: anger and fear, for example, act as signals to warn us of danger or discomfort. But we need to listen to the messages behind these emotions, express the negative feelings safely, act on them as necessary, and then let them go. Often, for a whole variety of reasons, we don't do any of these things. We try to pretend that our negative feelings do not exist and, by so doing, we turn them inwards. That's when they can manifest themselves as physical symptoms.

In the case of children, especially young children, they feel a whole range of emotions, but lack the experience to recognize and deal with them. Often, they can't begin to put a name to an emotion. So feelings of hurt, anger, sadness, jealousy and fear can swamp them and they are utterly powerless to control them.

The toddler tantrum is a good example of feelings out of control. Very often, the child will be frightened by the whole experience, and a calm, reassuring adult who doesn't fly off the handle is exactly what they need. Either that, or distraction or pure exhaustion will end the tantrum.

In children with special needs, negative feelings can be worsened by the inability to express them, by sensory issues, and by frustration at limited motor abilities. But the good thing is that flower and other homeopathic remedies are particularly effective in children. If you can work out the right remedies, problems such as nightmares, clinginess and crying can be instantly resolved.

Energy channels

The majority of complementary therapies look at the body in terms of energy flowing through it and around it. This energy is called different things, according to where the particular therapy originated. Western healing talks in terms of the 'aura', or the human energy field. It also talks of the universal energy field, and God. Broadly speaking, healers see all objects, including ourselves, as being part of an amazing sea of energy.

Indian therapies such as yoga call this energy 'prana', while Chinese therapies such as acupuncture, t'ai chi and qi gong call it 'chi' or 'qi', and Japanese therapies such as reiki call it 'ki'.

When the body is healthy and in balance, its energy field is unimpeded, and it works at its optimum. But many things, including infections, physical stresses and emotional stresses, can create blockages and depletions in the energy flow, leading ultimately to disease.

The 'hands-on' therapies, such as aromatherapy, healing, Indian head massage, kinesiology, osteopathy, reflexology, reiki and shiatsu, all address this energy flow through gentle hand movements over the body. And some 'hands-on' therapies, such as healing and reiki, can also be done through meditation and visualization when the patient is not even present.

Aromatherapy involves the use of essential plant oils which can have a powerful effect on the patient's emotions and physical health. They are applied sparingly through massage, or by letting the oils diffuse into the atmosphere by adding drops in a bowl of water gently heated over a tea light candle (or nightlight), or simply by sprinkling some drops into a hot bath.

Reflexology focuses on helping the whole body through massaging pressure points on the feet. Shiatsu is a type of acupressure, using finger pressure rather than needles (as in traditional acupuncture) to stimulate energy flow in blocked areas of the body.

Chiropractic is similar to osteopathy, but different in that it tends to focus on gently tweaking specific areas. Chiropractors make use of X-rays to help them understand the problem, whereas osteopaths tend to treat the whole body. Making much use of a technique called cranial osteopathy, osteopathic techniques for children are so gentle that you can scarcely see any movement in the practitioner's hands. But it can nevertheless have a profound effect, most visibly in terms of relaxing and calming a child, and raising his or her immunity.

Controlled movement

Another block of therapies are the movement therapies, such as yoga, qi gong and t'ai chi. These use stretches, slow movements, held postures and breathing to stimulate energy flow through the body, remove blockages and induce relaxation.

These therapies are not at first glance so suitable for children, and they're not commonly used for children with special needs, but they do have their uses. You can gently position young or immobile children into simple stretches, while older and more mobile children can start practising the movements alongside you. Children enjoy the exercises, and through them they get a greater sense of body awareness, which they may lack.

A balanced approach

When you are new to the idea of energy fields and energy blockages, it can all seem very difficult to understand or accept. Most of us have been brought up with a mechanistic view of our bodies: if a part goes wrong, we get that part fixed, usually by going to a doctor who gives us a drug or other treatment.

Conventional (orthodox) medicine can be excellent, especially in acute conditions; and many of us have had very positive experiences of conventional medicine. If you take your sick child to the doctor and you receive medication that works superbly, with no side-effects, and you feel calm, reassured and extremely happy after the visit, then the orthodox medicine is working marvellously for you and your child.

But if you keep returning to the doctor with the same complaint, and treatment either does nothing to help or actually seems to make things worse, then it can be worth considering alternatives.

It can also be worth getting into the habit of using complementary therapies to maintain good health, meaning that crisis visits to the GP or hospital become less likely.

Timmy's tale

I am definitely in favour of complementary therapy, as long as you choose suitably qualified practitioners. My son has ongoing osteopathy and homeopathy, and these two combined seem to work very well together. Let me tell you a little about our experience.

Timmy used to be somewhat sickly, always succumbing to infections. His appetite was poor, he was painfully thin, and he just didn't grow very much. During his worst bout of illness he developed a curvature of the spine.

He also had sensory processing problems that never seemed to be fully recognized by any of the many doctors we saw. Too much noise upset him; he was distressed by certain textures – he couldn't bear, for example, the feel of sand under his feet. He was sensitive to natural daylight, and the gentlest breeze seemed to upset him. He was extremely sensitive around his arms and hands, and preferred not to change position too much. None of these things can have helped his delayed development.

Conventional attempts to cure the infections seemed to depend on antibiotics, but we worried about the accumulative effect of these, especially since they gave him thrush and diarrhoea. Orthodox attempts to help him gain weight came down to dietary supplements such as Pediasure, a complete liquid food. But when he was on these his appetite seemed to become even worse, and his health did not improve.

And Timmy's sensory problems were hardly addressed by anybody, although as time went by and we learnt what to ask for, we did get help from occupational and other therapies.

So we took him to an osteopath, who used very gentle 'cranial' techniques. This seemed to help his immunity and improved his sensory problems to some extent. Then, on her advice, we added homeopathy. The type of homeopathy we opted for involves a diagnostic method called electro-acupuncture, which is reasonably common in some other European countries, but fairly new to Britain. It involves measuring the body's resistance to various toxins with the use of electrodes on the skin; it is a completely painless procedure.

The value of electro-acupuncture, according to its practitioners, is that actual infections can be identified and treated homeopathically. Our son was found to have toxoplasmosis, even though conventional medical tests had proved negative. Homeopaths who use this method believe that infections such as toxoplasmosis are a lot more common than conventional tests would suggest.

Doctors say that toxoplasmosis is only dangerous if contracted by a woman during or just before pregnancy, though they also say that, once caught, it can never be eradicated from the body. However, homeopaths say that if a woman contracts it years before she becomes pregnant, then it can still cause problems – and that it can cause problems in subsequent pregnancies also.

No fewer than three homeopaths we consulted told us that toxoplasmosis is a common cause of developmental delays and many other neurological problems, but they also said that it can be eradicated from the body homeopathically.

At first we found the difference between what the homeopaths and the doctors were saying to be bewildering. We were used to trusting in doctors, and yet their methods weren't helping our son. We knew that homeopathy is extremely gentle, and therefore we felt it was worth trying.

There was no instant cure; the whole process took time. But over the months and years, we have seen major improvements in our son's health. His appetite has become good, he is gaining weight, and he is hardly ever ill – he can go for a year or more at a time without antibiotics, which is wonderful.

Timmy's development is also coming along fast enough to impress his various conventional therapists. Despite his delays and his slender build, he's really just a normal, sociable little boy. And his spinal curvature, although still present, has stabilized – possibly even improved – against all medical predictions, as has his muscle tone. People have started asking us more about our methods, because they can see they are working.

The right therapy for you

You can probably tell from the above account that I would recommend osteopathy (using gentle cranial techniques) and homeopathy to any parent of a child with special needs. But your child's needs may well be different to mine, or certain practitioners may not be available where you live, or you may simply benefit from different therapies, or a different combination.

Here are some suggestions to help you get the right therapy for your child.

Consult your child's doctor

Complementary medicine is not supposed to replace conventional medicine. In fact, the two work best when they're used together. Good doctors know this, as do good complementary practitioners. If your doctor is not supportive, it may be worth changing to a doctor who is.

Nowadays, increasing numbers of doctors have some complementary expertise themselves. Others may have a homeopath or an osteopath running a clinic in their surgery, or can refer you to a good practitioner. Yet others may simply be able to act as a sounding board while you do the research to find the best therapies for your child.

Talk to other parents

Find out what has worked for other children with similar problems to those of your child; get personal recommendations from other parents. Ask at your local special needs centre. Contact the most relevant parents support group for your child's condition. You can do this through Contact a Family (see Appendix 1: Useful organizations). Do research on the internet: find other parents, and patients, who have tried the techniques you are considering for your child.

Start reading about it

There are increasing numbers of good books available in bookshops or through internet bookstores. An on-line bookshop such as amazon. co.uk is particularly useful for buying books from abroad – many of the best books happen to come from the USA. And, as internet bookstores don't have to maintain expensive high street outlets, most of their titles are discounted.

Or become a regular reader of a magazine such as *Here's Health*, which contains lots of personal experiences of the various therapies, is endorsed by a panel of experts from complementary and orthodox medicine, and also contains useful addresses for further information.

Contact accredited organizations for further information and/or practitioners. You can find these through the Henry Spink Trust, mentioned below.

Contact the Henry Spink Foundation

The Henry Spink Foundation (see Appendix 1: Useful organizations) is a good starting point for parents looking for information about complementary therapies and other treatments for their children. It was set up by a couple who have two children with special needs, and aims to give help without bias. It shares an office with Contact a Family.

Here is an e-mail about the Henry Spink Foundation's activities, sent to me by chairman and founder, Henrietta Spink:

We believe that the favourite therapies for children with special needs are: cranial osteopathy, osteopathy (they are regarded as safe therapies), homeopathy, aromatherapy, healing, reflexology.

We are not a medical organization and therefore cannot recommend any treatment or therapist but we give names of organizations where a list of therapists can be obtained. It is important that we remain unbiased.

When parents approach us with a specific condition we are keen to give them information on all therapies known as helpful for this condition (according to our research). We want to cover all the options available. We want to help parents who are faced with no diagnosis for their children, or when they are told that not a lot can

79

be done to improve their children's condition, by giving them names of organizations but also by giving them information on therapies (how they work, who for, research publications etc.) they may have never heard about.

We have fact sheets on therapies and can create fact sheets on treatments for specific disorders on request. Our tools are: the internet, books, magazines, libraries, documents, newspapers, info from organizations etc . . .

Make sure it's gentle

One thing that used to put me off complementary methods for my son was the fear factor; I worried that these methods might do more harm than good. In reality, complementary therapy for children is, and should be, extremely gentle. It shouldn't be invasive, or hurtful, or in any way upsetting for your child. In this respect it scores more highly than many orthodox techniques.

When I first, tentatively, took my baby to an osteopath (on the recommendation of his GP), I regretted not going sooner. As mentioned earlier in this chapter, osteopathy for children and babies involves incredibly gentle massage of the head and the rest of the body. This type is popularly called cranial osteopathy, but really it addresses the whole body. It can help with anything from fretful crying, to cerebral palsy and seizures. The sooner you begin, the more effective it can be.

Investigate affordable options

One of the great things about conventional medicine is that you can get it free. The same may not be true of complementary medicine, and many parents are put off because of this. They think, 'I can't afford it', and then forget the whole idea. But there are ways around this. Here are a few of them:

1 See if you can get it on the NHS. Ask your child's GP/consultant.
2 See if you can get it through medical insurance. If you or your partner has a health insurance scheme through your job, you may be able to put your child on it for a small amount extra every month, or you could just take out insurance yourself. Many insurers pay for complementary therapies, as long as the practitioner is accredited and has been practising for a certain number of years – conditions vary from insurer to insurer.

Insurers can also, incidentally, be a good source of information about accredited and long-established local practitioners.

3 See if you can get complementary therapy through a charity. You may, if you're lucky, find a local charity that will give you a grant to cover the costs – it's always worth asking and making your case. Or you may find a charity that provides subsidized therapy. The Osteopathic Centre for Children in London (see Appendix 1: Useful organizations) is a notable example. The Centre suggests a subsidized fee, but if you can't afford even this, you can get the treatment anyway.

4 See if you can learn some simple methods yourself. You may be able to go on a day, weekend or evening course at your local college: aromatherapy, Bach flower remedies, healing, reflexology and yoga are all listed in my local college prospectus. Also, my local college offers Indian head massage, a simple technique that one mother recently highly recommended to me.

Three golden rules

1 Always make sure that any practitioner you consult is suitably qualified, and that you feel comfortable with him or her. Bear in mind that a good complementary practitioner always works alongside, and not in opposition to, conventional medicine.

2 Remember that the experts – conventional or complementary – do not always get it right. You are the real expert on your child.

3 Follow your instincts – do what feels right for you and your child.

The healer in you

You don't always have to go to the experts. You have the means within you to help your child feel better, and there are simple methods you can use at home to help with your child's health problems.

The great things about home healing are that it's free, it's easy, and it works. If you're not used to this kind of approach, read on with an open mind. Try the suggestions you feel most comfortable with. Over time, you will evolve your own methods, because we are all different, and we all find the ways that suit us best. (You'll find some good home healing books listed in Appendix 3: Further reading.)

Look after yourself

This is the first rule. In order to look after others, you first must look after yourself. This means listening to your body and responding to its messages. Eat nourishing foods when you're hungry, rest when you're tired. I know this is often easier said than done. At the very least, register what you're feeling and try to do something about it later in the day when you do have a moment.

When you're feeling stressed, find ways of relaxing – such as a bath, or some gentle yoga exercises. Every day, go for a walk and look around you. Really drink in the colours of the natural world: the flowers, berries, fruits and leaves.

Take a few minutes several times a day just to close your eyes and relax. Concentrate on your breathing; think of nothing else. Or paint a picture in your mind of somewhere, real or imaginary, that you find particularly beautiful and relaxing. It might be a tranquil, scented garden, or a heavenly tropical beach with the salty waves lapping gently over white coral sand. Feel the warm water and the softly crunching sand between your toes.

This kind of pleasurable daydreaming is instantly relaxing, and it serves another purpose too. As you do more of it and your imagination becomes stronger, you will become better at visualization. And visualization, as we shall see, is one of the most useful tools for the home healer.

Get into the habit of valuing yourself, and your body. Take pleasure in eating delicious healthy foods, and drinking healthy drinks. Exert your body in pleasurable ways. Don't become a health fiend though – eating a strict diet and embarking on a punishing fitness routine. The idea is to enjoy yourself, and to grow naturally into a healthier state as a result of that relaxed enjoyment. If you're a few pounds overweight, don't berate yourself for it. Try to love yourself as you are.

Create a happy, peaceful atmosphere at home

We all know how houses have their own distinctive atmospheres. Often, these develop unconsciously, but we can consciously look around and make changes to make the home feel better. Here are a few suggestions.

Walk through each of your rooms, looking at them afresh. Do you like what you see? If you don't, start making changes. Give away things you don't like, or no longer use. Remove clutter as much as possible: put toys in a big, inviting box. For semi-mobile children, place a few in strategic corners.

If you possibly can, start viewing housework as a calming activity in its own right. Put on some favourite music and enjoy the feeling that you're clearing away old dirt, creating new order. Do it at an enjoyable pace; don't rush about like a mad thing, so desperate to finish that you're only half-aware of what you're doing.

In your living room, rearrange ornaments in groups of colours so that individual areas are harmonious. Concentrate on creating corners of beauty so that you will be able to look at a shelf or a mantelpiece and like what you see.

If your child's problems include wrecking the house, you can still create corners of beauty, though they will have to be higher up and out of reach. You could follow the example of one family, which has put family portraits in beautiful frames and grouped them in pleasing collections on the walls. Another family has collections of beautiful landscapes on their walls. Lower down, they've put warmly coloured rugs on the floor, and bright cushions on the sofas.

Buy a large, long-burning candle and light it every evening. The glow is calming, and you can spend a little time imagining that the small amount of smoke produced is carrying away negative energies from the day – out of the room, through an open window. Vary the candles over time: use scented ones, tea lights, floating ones, whatever appeals.

Light an incense stick in the evening to serve the same purpose. As with candles, buy in bulk if you can because it's much cheaper that way. My local Buddhist shop sells boxes containing hundreds of Japanese incense sticks for around £12, which last for well over a year. You don't have to be a Buddhist to enjoy them; the scent is instantly calming.

Look around your home: is there a lot of medical equipment related to your child's condition? If there is, do you feel comfortable with this? Many parents and children do not like looking at orthopaedic equipment. You may be able to put some away; or you may be able to send some back and instead use things you have around the home. Spend a little time thinking up ingenious solutions.

When contemplating new medical equipment, consider its aesthetic value. This is not frivolous: it really does matter. If a room has to contain a lot of hard, ugly, grey medical equipment, consider other ways in which you can improve the room: through bright soft cushions and drapes, wall posters, gentle lighting, music. Fasten a few cheeky cuddly toys on to the medical equipment – anything to soften the austere lines.

Collect your own kit of home remedies

What you put in your kit will depend on you. Maybe you know a few simple remedies that your mother passed on to you, and that she got from her mother. Maybe your child's complementary practitioner has recommended something to you. Maybe you've found a good book on home remedies in the library, and have written the best ones in a notebook.

What you need depends very much on your own child's circumstances. Make sure you use things suitable for his or her age and condition. Some things work for some people, but not for others. Be aware that although home remedies are generally safe, many of them have not been through exhaustive clinical trials.

Especially if your child is on medication, you must check with his or her doctor. To give one example, an article in the *British Medical Journal* recently stated that echinacea, a popular herbal remedy for boosting the immune system, can react badly with steroids. Never give your child anything that makes you feel uncomfortable.

Here are some of the things in my home remedy kit that I have found effective for my son, and the whole family. All the items listed can be bought in high street chemists and health shops:

- *Bach flower remedies.* As described earlier in this chapter, these are gentle homeopathic preparations that address emotional upsets such as nightmares and clinginess.

  To choose the right treatments, it's worth buying one of the little books that are commonly sold beside the remedies, and studying it carefully. A good basic preparation is Rescue Remedy, a combination of five remedies that can help soothe and reassure during times of stress and trauma. These might include hospital appointments and exams.

  Other specific flower remedies in my kit include mimulus (recommended for fearful children) and honeysuckle (good for banishing traumatic memories).
- *Echinacea.* A herbal tincture that can be extremely effective in nipping upper respiratory infections in the bud, or helping them pass more quickly and not so severely (see note of caution above).

- *Arnica*. A homeopathic remedy available in cream or tablet form. It is an effective treatment for bruises and shock.
- *Floradix*. The children's version is called Kindervital. It's a food supplement that your child can take by spoon or in a beaker. It contains lots of natural plant and fruit extracts as well as calcium and vitamins A, B, C, D and E. It's sweetened with maple syrup, and it tastes nice!
- *Probiotics*. These are sometimes branded as acidophilus, which is just one of the main varieties of probiotic. They are beneficial bacteria that are found naturally in the intestine and aid digestion. They are found in yoghurt, especially live yoghurt, but available in larger quantities in capsule form. It's best to keep most varieties in the fridge. They are especially useful after a course of antibiotics, which diminishes natural probiotic levels in the body, and also after any illness causing an upset stomach, or a change of diet, or travel.
- *Aromatherapy oils*. These are helpful (but must always be used externally) in soothing a child through a variety of ills or just to increase well-being. I'd definitely advise reading up about this, so you can use them safely and effectively. Only some sorts are suitable for babies, for example. And you should never use them undiluted on the skin (except lavender, in certain situations), as they are extremely concentrated.

You can put two drops of oil in a room diffuser, or a few drops on a tissue on a warm radiator. Or you can add a couple of drops to the bath – for younger children, disperse the oil in a small amount of milk first. I have also placed a few drops on a tissue and tied it securely close to my son's bed at night, but out of reach of grasping fingers.

These are my favourite oils:

- *Tea tree*: a powerful antiviral, antibiotic and antiseptic. A couple of drops in a bath, morning and night, can really help to stamp out an infection. Can also be used as a disinfectant for dishcloths, in the wash, or on kitchen surfaces.
- *Lavender*: also good for infections, as well as headaches and burns (put a small amount neat on a burn and blisters are far less likely to form). It smells wonderful too.

  Apart from the oil, you can get lavender in the form of a gel, or water, that you can dab on hot foreheads to soothe and cool.
- *Eucalyptus*: good for clearing the nose, and helps to fight colds.
- *Geranium*: promotes happiness and well-being.
- *Lemon*: fresh and invigorating.

Simple home therapies

These are all very important in restoring or maintaining good health.

Laughter

It's good practice to check the laughter quotient in your house. Is your child laughing every day? Are you? Are the other members of the family? Laughter is immensely curative. If your house is short of laughter, start bringing more in through silly games, tickling, comedy programmes on television, funny books. Get into the habit of seeing the lighter side of life, and sharing it with your family.

Colour

Give some thought to the colours you habitually dress your child in, as well as the colours of his or her room and bedclothes. We all know how bright colours can be uplifting, natural colours can be calming, while murky colours can be depressing.

Many healers make big use of colour in their work – in particular, the seven colours of the rainbow. According to healers, each colour has particular qualities. However, your own and your child's feelings about individual colours will reveal more than any list devised by others. Just get into the habit of noting your feelings about colours – and responding to them.

When dressing your child on a daily basis, if a colour feels right to your child and to you, go for it. If you hate a colour, then it's not right for that particular day. Certain colours may feel right on certain days, while others feel right on others. Go with your child's preferences, and yours. Below I've listed some of the commonly accepted meanings of particular colours:

- Red is energizing, recharging and warming, good for energy and helping us to feel 'connected' to the physical world around us.
- Orange is energizing, balancing and harmonizing.
- Yellow is linked with logical thinking, communication and joy.
- Green is linked with emotions, growth, life energy and healing.
- Blue is calming, peaceful and linked with deeper knowledge.
- Indigo is concerned with intuition, insights and vision.
- Violet is concerned with the spiritual realm and transformation.

If you notice particular colours cropping up in dreams about your child, take note of how those colours make you feel and what their message might be.

One mother, for example, dreamed that her child's doctor reached for a big jar, high up on a shelf, and passed it to her. The jar contained a yellow substance and was labelled 'Sunshine'. She decided the dream was simply telling her to let her daughter spend more time outdoors, in natural sunlight. After a few weeks of spending more time outdoors, the mother noticed that her daughter was really thriving and had a bloom to her.

Massage

Never underestimate the power of gentle therapeutic touch. You can use a simple oil, such as sweet almond oil; or read up about aromatherapy, and then add oils that are suitable for your child.

If your child enjoys this, give regular all-over massages. Or simply give foot massages, with occasional fuller massages. Foot massages are very soothing, and can make people feel good all over. You don't have to know all about reflexology points – but if you do, it's a bonus.

Basically, just use your intuition: cup the feet gently in your hands. Rub each foot firmly so it doesn't tickle, but not too hard. Use slow, calming movements. Feel peaceful while you're doing it.

Social contact

We all need contact with other people – and that includes your child with special needs. Make an effort to create a good social life for yourself and the whole family. Pick up the phone and invite someone over. Review your child's social contacts, whether they be nursery, school, or just local friends. Is he happy with these? Does he come home troubled? If any particular environment is not making him socially happy, consider finding out why and, if necessary, moving him to a different nursery, school or whatever.

Stimulation

We all thrive on novelty. Periodically review how stimulating and varied your child's life is. Can you bring in some welcome changes? Can you play more games with your child; encourage all your children to play together with some artful new ideas from you; bring in some fresh new games?

Rest

As soon as your child looks pale and tired, let her rest, even if that just means a cuddle, a drink and a book with you on the sofa.

If your child becomes ill, don't put her back into school or nursery before she's ready. Convalescence used to be highly prized, but nowadays, in our fast-paced society, we seem to think we can do without it. However, convalescence does serve a valuable purpose, giving your child a chance to recharge her batteries and raise her immunity before the next possible onslaught of infection.

If your child is ill, a fun idea is to buy one or more little presents, wrap them loosely in bright tissue paper, and give them to her with much fanfare. Everyone loves presents, and they don't have to cost much. Make sure you spend time with your child playing with the little gifts. Your company is the most healing thing of all.

Calm in a crisis

When your child is ill, there can be a temptation to worry, panic and fear, but one of the hardest lessons for any parent to learn is that ongoing fear can do more harm than good. If your child is very ill, this still holds true: somehow, you have to let go of fear and project feelings of love, warmth and reassurance.

Of course, fear serves a purpose: it tells us something is wrong. Therefore, our anxiety should be listened to. Fear may be a signal to call the doctor, or go immediately to the hospital, or just to put your child straight to bed with a cuddle and a warm drink. But whatever the situation, once you've listened to the message from your fear and acted accordingly, you have to let it go and concentrate on being a strong, helpful support for your child.

Little things like holding your child and making sure your breathing is slow and relaxed can make a big difference to his or her comfort levels. Actively try to project a sense of calm, the feeling that your child is being looked after.

Prayer

You don't have to go to church, or even necessarily practise any particular religion, in order to pray. You can do it silently, so no one need even know you're doing it. Prayer is a useful, comforting aid to the person who prays and for the person who is being prayed for; and many people believe that it does make a real difference. So whatever your religious beliefs, or lack of them, it can be very worthwhile to keep an open mind, accept the presence of (or at least the possibility of) a universal consciousness or power, and simply pray.

In the best sort of prayer you don't become too specific. After all, none of us knows exactly what sort of healing another person really wants or needs. So in your prayer give thanks for the many good things in your life. Give thanks for your child and appreciate his special qualities. Feel gratitude for the gifts he has brought you. Perhaps he has brought you love and laughter and new lessons in compassion. Think about these.

Ask for him, and you, to be open to healing. Ask for the healing to enter him and work on him in the ways that he really needs. Then sit for a few moments, just thinking about this. Be receptive to any thoughts that come to you during this time. Be open to a sense of peace and love, and feel your connection with all living things.

Visualization

This, combined with prayer, is one of the most useful methods I have discovered of helping a child towards good health. Broadly, in visualization you use the power of your imagination to intuit what's wrong with your child, and/or you use your mind to envisage your child becoming whole and well again. That's all you do: it's very easy.

If you are new to the idea, you may think it's hocus pocus – how can thinking about something actually create it? But the world is a lot more mysterious than we often think. We are linked in invisible ways to other people, especially to those whom we love, and our thoughts can influence their well-being.

You only have to think about the dark vibes that emanate from a troubled person to realize what I mean. Or think about how good you feel in the presence of a genuinely kind and peaceful person.

Visualization is increasingly practised by adults with serious health problems such as cancer; and parents are beginning to use it with their children too. There are many books on the subject (see Appendix 3: Further reading), but here are some straightforward exercises to get you started. I suggest you simply read them now, get a feel for them, and then use them or adapt them later as you wish. It's not meant to be hard work. Just sit or lie somewhere comfortable, relax, close your eyes, and let your mind do the rest.

Pink doorway

Take three deep breaths and feel yourself relaxing. With every inbreath, imagine healing golden light entering you. With every outbreath, imagine dark negative energies and bad feelings leaving you and passing harmlessly away.

When you have relaxed in this way, imagine that you see a pink oval in front of you. You walk towards it. As you approach, you realize that it's the size of a door. Before you enter, stop a moment. Review the central question in your mind. Perhaps it concerns your child's health. Perhaps you want to know what's wrong with her, and how you can help her to feel better.

Now enter that pink oval doorway. As you slowly pass through, feel the remaining bad energies in your body being cleaned away, leaving you calm and relaxed. And now, step through.

You find yourself in a different place. Let your imagination supply the picture without any effort from you. Perhaps you're on a mountainside; or by a woodland stream; or on a beach; or in a lush green field with a wide view over the sea.

In front of you is your child. Let your mind conjure her up without too much effort from you. It is possible that you will see her in a situation you may not expect to see. Remember, this is just your imagination giving you a picture of something you have already intuited about your child. It's not actually happening.

For example, you may see her covered in little bugs and you then realize that the main problem that needs addressing right now is an infection. Or perhaps it's an old infection that has never quite cleared up.

Now, in your mind, imagine that the bugs are leaving your child. They are floating off and away into the sky. As they float far away, they become transformed. They glow and then fade, and then just become part of the universal energy – no longer harmful, just neutral.

Become aware that your child needs loving energy from you to restore her to full health. Imagine that at the centre of you there is a warm sun or furnace of molten energy, connecting you to the universe. From that sun, you can pluck what you need. Perhaps you pluck a cup or bottle of some golden, healing substance. In your mind, give it to your child. As she drinks, see the warm, healing light enter and fill her. See her becoming radiant with health.

When you feel like doing so, walk back to the pink oval door. As you pass through this door, again feel any negative energies leaving you. In your mind, you then step through into the real world and open your eyes.

You can do this as often as you like. If your child is ill, you may find yourself doing it every day for a few days. You will find that the pictures you imagine naturally change. But remember you are always working towards a picture of radiant, glowing good health. Start thinking of your child regularly as having radiant good health.

Healing light

This is something you can do when you're cuddling your child before he goes to bed, or perhaps while giving him a massage. Or while you're giving him a quick hug. But you don't have to have physical contact to do it: he could be miles away. It's incredibly calming, and your child may sleep very well after it.

As you breathe in, imagine that you are breathing in a golden, healing energy from the universe. Feel yourself filling up with this golden light as you breathe in deeply.

Then, as you breathe out, imagine the healing golden light is entering your child. If you're massaging, cuddling or hugging him, imagine the golden energy travelling through your hands and into his body. If you're not, simply visualize it spreading through his whole body, filling him with radiant, healing energy.

Do this for several breaths, until you feel that you and he have both been sufficiently bathed in this healing energy. And then imagine that it will continue its healing work over the next few hours, or through the night, making your child well.

As a variation, you can imagine that you are breathing into him each of the colours of the rainbow in turn. Each colour contains a different type of healing energy to help your child. It can help to visualize each colour in terms of real things, such as those listed below. As you do this, be aware of how your child is connected to nature all around him, and how he gains strength and energy from that connection:

Red: roses, rubies, the red sky at night
Orange: oranges, marigolds
Yellow: lemons, primroses, daffodils
Green: leaves, grass, emeralds
Blue: a dazzling, clear blue sky
Indigo: blue-mauve flowers, lapis lazuli, the evening sky
Violet: amethyst, passionflowers.

As a very quick variation, at night or when saying goodbye, you can blow your child a kiss and imagine that you're blowing the golden healing light all around him, so it will surround and protect him like an aura all night long. Or blow a kiss and imagine the light as a rainbow.

Pink clouds of light

This is a very useful visualization to improve your relationship with your partner.

You can do this exercise in just a few seconds or minutes. Sit

91

comfortably, take a few deep breaths, and feel yourself relaxing. Close your eyes. Now, imagine that you are immersed in and surrounded by pink clouds of light. In your mind's eye, you look across to your partner, who is also glowing with clouds of pink light.

Now, imagine that the pink light from you and your partner reaches out and meets between the two of you. Long, constantly changing tendrils of pink cloudy light are dancing between you, making shapes, meeting, and changing and touching again. Be aware of a loving feeling within you and between the two of you. Be aware that the pink light is a manifestation of that loving feeling. When you feel ready, open your eyes and return to the present.

You can practise visualization any time that you like. It doesn't matter if you don't believe in it – just treat it as an exercise of the imagination. Once you start, you will probably continue, because it brings immediate benefits of calm, and can act as a wonderful antidote – for example, to bad feelings following a medical appointment. In the long term, the positive thinking it engenders can make a noticeable difference to your child. Try it and see.

6

Your older child

Many parents of children with special needs agree that life becomes easier after the first few years. Your child's condition may improve, and/or your ability to cope gets better. But parents of older children also say that every period of transition can bring up the old fears, sadness and worries all over again.

Here's how one parent describes the experience of adjusting over the years. Annie Cawthorn is the mother of 11-year-old Peter, who has a lovely sunny personality, but is held back by microcephaly, quadriplegia, sight impairment and associated delays. Annie is also the co-ordinator of the Microcephaly Support Group, and a real inspiration to other parents of children with health problems. She is honest about her own feelings, and helps others to feel that what they're doing matters.

In a recent newsletter Annie wrote the following:

My son Peter will be going to secondary school this autumn. Suddenly, all the support systems we had in place at primary school mean nothing any more. We have to start again, in a new environment, with new people. There are worries about how Peter will adjust to his new school, and the new routine.

And at the same time, we are facing the fact that Peter is getting bigger and we must change our house around to suit his changing needs. We are planning to move his bedroom downstairs into what is currently the kitchen – the heart of the house – and build a small extension to accommodate a new kitchen and dining area.

It seems to me that we've come full circle. When your child is first diagnosed, you're devastated, and at the bottom of a steep learning curve. Over time, you learn to cope. But then you reach a new stage in your child's life and you feel unhappy and have to learn to cope all over again. We will eventually adjust to these changes, but getting there, as we all know, is tough.

What helps? Talking about it does: putting your thoughts into words for the first time, recognizing that this is what you're feeling, sharing the burden with others.

At every new stage in our children's lives, we have to rise to the challenge. When a child starts at primary school, secondary school, when he leaves home ... these are scary times for any parent, but undeniably tougher for us because we are so conscious of our children's vulnerability. We feel an overpowering need to protect our children while giving them the means to an independent life.

If our child's condition is long term, at every stage we may also have a new phase of mourning to complete: for the normal life we feel we have lost.

When I talk to parents of older children, I'm aware of two things. First, how wise they are, and how reassuring. They have navigated many difficult stretches of parenthood, and have learnt many skills. Often they have strengths that only come with experience, and the willingness to learn from that experience.

The second thing I notice is that this is a field that is changing quite rapidly. A few years ago, when these parents were at the start of their own learning curves, things were probably more depressing. A child's potential was deemed less. If she had a problem, she was more likely to have a problem for life. Also, there weren't nearly as many support groups for parents, so they were more likely to feel isolated and left to find their own solutions.

A few decades ago, the situation was even worse: children with special needs were routinely segregated by being put into special schools. Children who had physical problems but no learning difficulties were given inadequate academic schooling. Their prospects for normal lives and careers were significantly lower.

In previous years, people without experience of special needs were frequently prejudiced, believing that such children were capable of little. It was an era in which people rarely acknowledged their own weaknesses, and certainly did not tolerate any in others.

If you, like me, are the parent of a younger child with special needs, you are in a much better situation than the parents who have gone before us. They have paved the way for us, made it easier. Due to their efforts, we expect more for our children: more intervention, more potential.

All around us, society is changing. Prejudice is gradually melting away. Even though each of us may find our hackles regularly rise at some hurtful comment or unconscious insult, overall we are perhaps more likely to encounter everyday kindness from neighbours and strangers. We are more likely to be treated as normal parents of normal children who just happen to have health problems.

In this improving environment, we may become a little less defensive, though of course we still have our moments! And we are probably more likely to consider complementary therapies and home healing methods, both of which can make a significant difference to our children's day-to-day well-being and eventual outcome.

In these ways, we are lucky, because the future is ours. Or, to be more precise, our children's. And the better we deal with every new stage, the better it is for our children.

If you are reading this as the parent of an older child, you are just as much part of these improvements. Every single one of our children, whatever his or her age, has the potential today to do far better than in previous eras.

How to choose the best school for your child

Mainstream or special – which do you prefer? The government has a policy of giving as many children as possible inclusive education – that is, education in a mainstream school, with extra support provided as required.

Many parents welcome this; it makes a lot of sense. The aim is for our children to enjoy as full a role as possible in society, and they are more likely to do that if, from the start, they are a part of the community.

There is another argument, which I like, that says that our children actually have something to contribute to a mainstream school. At the very least, they can teach other children about compassion, empathy and tolerance. Each child has a unique personality that can add to the community; he or she can give something to others.

But other parents feel that a mainstream school is just too difficult for their children, and that a special school may help – at least for a while. The crucial thing is that it's you, the parent, who has the biggest say, because you are the one who best knows your child's own preferences. Is he content in a mainstream situation, with support as necessary? Or is he happier in a more controlled environment?

Some parents find that health and educational professionals try to persuade them towards special schools. One parent adviser I spoke to says there is an invisible line that health professionals observe. This line is impossible to define, and it certainly doesn't officially exist, but if your child's needs are deemed to fall below the invisible line, they will try to persuade you to send him or her to a special school.

On the other hand, it's possible that we can become too defensive about this. We hear bad stories from other parents, we fear the worst, and assume it will happen to us. But everyone's story is different. If we go into all this with a clear idea of what we want, and are able to communicate it, then it is likely that we will get it.

As always, do the research. Contact specialist groups that can offer you advice. If you want mainstream education for your child, one very useful group is Parents for Inclusion (see Appendix 1: Useful organizations), which runs local support groups and a national telephone helpline. They suggest that we are more likely to get inclusive schooling for our children if we bear the following points in mind:

- We feel OK about our own feelings, perhaps by having talked them through with others.
- We feel positive and proud of our child.
- We decide what we want and approach the whole process with that in mind. That means, for example, in meetings with the educational psychologist who has been assigned to assess our child for a statement of special educational needs (more of which below), we state clearly that we would like our child to have mainstream education, with particular support.

Parents and professionals sometimes become heated in the area of education. Things can get political. To keep your head in the midst of it all, bear in mind Annie Cawthorn's advice: 'It's easy to get on a bandwagon and commit yourself either to the cause of inclusive education, or to the cause of special schools. But the most important question you need to ask is this: where will your child be happiest?' When you're clear about that, everything else falls into place.

Here is a quick summary of things to bear in mind when considering individual schools for your child:

- Visit each of the schools on your shortlist in advance, and have a tour of the classrooms. Meet the head teacher if possible. She or he is the most influential person in the school. The way she comes across can tell you many things about the way the school is now, and the way it will be changing in the future. Notice details like her body language and general air, how well she copes with questions, and whether she knows the names of the children that you encounter on your tour.
- Consider all the sensory aspects: is the school an attractive space for children to work and grow in? Is it bright and cheerful? Is the noise level OK for your child?

- Will your child find it easy to get around the school? For example, if he has limited mobility, it helps a lot if the whole school is built on one level.
- Are parents actively encouraged to get involved, perhaps by coming in to help with reading, maths or other activities? Steve Moody, whose son Michael has a cranio-facial condition, goes into his children's school every week to help with reading. 'It's a good chance to see your child in the context of his peers,' he explains. 'Without this kind of involvement, a large part of my children's lives would be virtually unknown. I'd recommend any parent to volunteer in this way.'
- Do you like the general atmosphere of the school? Do children seem happy and involved? Do you feel welcome?
- Is there a sense of creativity in the school, in the form of art, music, dance and other areas?
- Does the head teacher talk in terms of helping individual children at the level they are at?
- What are the grounds like? Are there spaces for different types of outdoor play, including quiet nature areas, and good-quality, safe climbing frames?
- If you were a child again, would you like to be a pupil at the school?

Going for a statement

Around one in five of all school-age children are deemed to have special needs at any one time. Many of these are minor and/or temporary and can largely be met by the special-needs teacher and other specialists based at the school.

For around 2 per cent of schoolchildren, their needs are deemed great enough to warrant issuing a statement of special educational needs, also known as an SEN, which legally ensures their needs will be met. This is reassessed on an annual basis and a child continues to have a statement for as long as is necessary.

The whole process is often called 'statementing', which to many parents sounds awful. Parents and health professionals do often shudder a bit when talking about the statementing process – it has a bad reputation in terms of being time-consuming, and is a rich source of dissension among the many individuals involved in it.

But the statementing process doesn't have to be that bad. As a parent half-way through the process, I've been pleasantly surprised by the efficiency and friendliness of the people involved. It helps to bear in mind that everyone wants your child to benefit in the end, and the more clear you are in your dealings with professionals, the more likely you are to get what you want.

It's a good idea to communicate all the way along. Tell your child's therapists and portage worker what your aims are. Ask them if they feel happy about supporting those aims. Talk it over with them, listening to their views, giving yours. Having every single professional involved with your child write broadly similar recommendations in their reports clearly makes a big difference to the outcome. Remember, too, that you see each report and can suggest amendments.

It also helps to be clear about the faults of the statementing system. It can seem to go on for ages, with a whole range of specialists giving carefully worded reports which are then put into a draft statement, which you and everyone else will review, and then alterations are incorporated and the final statement is issued. Acronyms and jargon are liberally used throughout, making the process seem impenetrable, and somehow not quite in the real world for the parents.

Another thing that makes statementing horrible is the fact that you would rather not be doing it at all. If you are still raw and hurting about your child's problem, every step in the process will seem like a new wound. Later on, when you have had time to adjust and adapt, it will be considerably easier.

For this reason alone, I think it makes sense not to enter into the process too early. Unfortunately, if your child has obvious problems, health professionals tend to harp on about statementing from an early stage. There is a generally held view that the process is long and complex and therefore you should start as soon as possible.

But there is a legal requirement that every statement must be completed within 26 weeks. If you start the whole process one year before your child is due to go to school (or nursery school, if you are likely to need extra help there), then you are giving yourself plenty of time.

There is another reason why it makes sense not to do it too early: your child is changing all the time. Even if the changes seem small right now, we have to remember that every child has the potential for growth and development spurts.

At the same time, you don't want to leave it until the last minute, because ultimately the statement is all about getting your child the vital help that will benefit him or her. Viewed in this way, a statement is simply a means to help your child grow, learn and progress with ease towards eventual independence, which is just what education should be about for every child.

Whether your child is going to a mainstream or special school is irrelevant to the process of statementing – though in the final statement the school will be specified.

There are some distinct advantages to having a statement. Provided the school you wish your child to go to can cater for your child's needs, with specified outside help as laid out in the statement, it cannot refuse your child for any reasons outside their normal admission requirements. In this respect, a statement gives your child greater protection.

And schools can find them reassuring, because items on a statement don't come out of their budget. A child without a statement, who needs a lot of school resources to help him cope, can cost the school more than it can comfortably afford. In school budgeting terms, a child with a statement is a child of financial means.

There are three ways to get the statementing process started:

1 You can apply for it yourself, by writing a letter to the Special Educational Needs Officer at your local education authority. In your letter you don't need to go into too many details. You simply request a statutory assessment of special needs for your child. You give his or her name, age, and the month and year your child will be starting school.

   You can mention your child's diagnosis, or give a very brief description of his situation – global delays, or whatever. If he is at a nursery you can mention that here, and if he has intervention, such as occupational therapy, speech therapy, physiotherapy, portage, a one-to-one helper funded by a local charity at nursery, you can mention those too.

   One advantage of getting the ball rolling yourself is that you feel you are being proactive, in control, which always feels good.

2 Your child's community paediatrician can refer your child. He or she will discuss this with you before doing so.

3 If your child is already at school, his or her teacher will first approach the school's Special Educational Needs Co-ordinator, also known as SENCO. Together they will draw up a special plan of targets for your child, known as an Individual Education Plan, or IEP. This IEP will be reviewed regularly.

If your child does not meet these targets, then outside help, in the form of an educational psychologist and/or specialist teacher, may be brought in. If your child is considered to need it, a statutory assessment for a statement will be requested. You can request this directly, as in point 1 above. Obviously, you would do this in consultation with your child's teacher. At every stage of the process, it helps to view your child's teachers and other helpers as members of your child's team.

If your child clearly needs a statement, then this can be requested immediately, without going through the IEP stages.

At every stage of the process, you have rights. You have the right to see the draft statement and make comments; and you have the right to agree to an assessment, or not to agree to it. You also have the right to get help and advice from someone independent – the local education authority or school must tell you of a suitable person, such as a Parent Partnership adviser.

Coping at school

Here are some of the things that parents worry about:

1 That other children will laugh at or bully their child with special needs.
2 That he will be left floundering without the help he needs.
3 That his strengths will be ignored (especially if he's in a special school) and he won't get the real education he deserves.

Points 2 and 3 can be dealt with through the statementing process, and by constant liaison between you and your child's teachers. It's up to you to promote your child's strengths and make sure they are met. It's up to you, and the statementing process, to ensure that he does receive the help he needs.

Point 1 is a more subtle area. All parents worry about their child or children at school, whether they have special needs or not. We all want our children to mix happily with their peers. And we all know how children can target those who are different.

Reassuringly, there are plenty of parents who can describe positive experiences of their child at school. The key seems to be to let the other children know about your child's disabilities or learning difficulties. 'Kids ridicule what they don't understand,' says one mother. Once they know, they tend to become understanding, even protective.

One mother wrote to an on-line support group about her son's school

experiences: 'He's made a lot of friends, he's become more independent, and children treat him like any other kid, only more on a delicate/
understanding level.'

Another parent advised that you 'go in with sugar, rather than
vinegar'. That is, instead of being defensive or angry, you make a point
of being friendly to the other children. Tell them about your child's
condition in a natural, unforced way, and give them an opportunity to
ask questions. Help them to see that everyone is different, and that
differences can be OK – even good – because they make us who we
are.

Celebrate differences

This is a key point: differences are acceptable, but in our educational
system a great deal of emphasis is placed on being able to conform. To
be effective members of society we do have to learn how to fit in with
others, but to contribute to society – and to actually make a difference
– we do need to make the most of our own special qualities.

Sometimes that means we don't entirely conform. This is something
that many children with special needs discover.

So if, for example, your daughter lives in a fantasy world, always
spinning stories, she might alarm her teachers, but she could turn out to
be the next Jane Austen! If your son was late talking and unable to read
until the age of seven, he might turn out to be the next Einstein.

Or if your son swears that he can see colours when he hears sounds
(a condition known as synaesthesia, in which two or more senses are
neurologically connected to one another) then he might turn out to be
the next Rimsky-Korsakov or Liszt, who saw their musical composi-
tions in colour.

Of course, the vast majority of children with special needs do not
turn out to be geniuses, but every child has strengths that can be
appreciated, even celebrated.

Take Jessica, a 17-year-old who is totally dependent on others for all
her daily needs. Yet over the years her mother Vickie has come to
realize that Jessica has strengths that stand her in good stead. Vickie
writes:

Maybe the way we look at the world may need some changing. I
look at Jess and see a happy and loving child. Who is to say her way
of living or thinking is wrong or bad? What is the goal in life but to
be happy, loved, and feel good about yourself and others?

Well, Jess has all these qualities. I know a lot of people (like my parents) feel so bad for Jess but I try to turn it around and say, 'Yes, her life is going down a different path but maybe that path is OK too.'

Jessica is unusual because the brightness and alertness in her eyes do not correlate with her abilities. She is so aware – so interactive with people yet she does not show her intelligence in conventional ways. I always think that Jessica's gift is social. People who spend time with her fall in love with her and she is quite lucky because she needs people to support her in daily life skills. People enjoy helping a person that they enjoy, so Jess is fortunate in that regard.

Appreciating a child's strengths is important, because if we don't they can end up unhappy and frustrated, which can lead to behavioural problems. If we recognize and encourage strengths, while still spending time helping weaker areas, a child has a better chance of achieving his or her full potential.

Looking to the future

As our children grow older, all the coping strategies we've had to learn in the early years really do pay off. At the beginning, it was tougher – we had to work much harder than the average parent. But the good parenting techniques that we've acquired are invaluable in later years. In some ways, they give us an advantage over parents who never had to learn the skills we now know.

If, for example, we have learned to give time to our young children, listening to them without judgement, when they grow older they will probably keep on talking to us about things on their minds. As they become more independent, and their actions are less within our control, this trust becomes invaluable.

And if we have concentrated on building our children's confidence in their early years, they will be more able to cope with anything that comes their way. For example, we have already discussed how one of the things that parents worry about when their children are more vulnerable is bullying. Yet one of the best defences against bullying is social ease, which comes about via learning how to play, and talk, and generally connect with peers.

If we have made a point, from the start, of having an active social life at a level that suits our children, then we have helped them to be good mixers for the rest of their lives. This applies whatever their health problems, whatever their delays.

The good parenting practices that help your child with special needs are actually no different from the practices that help all children. They include: listening to your child; giving her choices; negotiating when appropriate; giving her a sense of power and independence, helping her to understand what other people are thinking and feeling, and thus helping her to build good relationships; giving her your unconditional love and support, and the space and freedom to be herself.

Ultimately, these practices all come down to one thing: treating your child with the respect that he or she, and every human being, deserves. When you bear these basic priorities in mind, all the practical decisions that may have to be made in the future become much easier.

You can make a difference

There is one final point to make. We didn't consciously choose to have a child with health, developmental or educational problems. But the experience of having a child with special needs does bring its own extraordinary benefits, if we are receptive to them, and open to changing our approach to life. By the time our children are older, we will have learned some valuable skills. Here are some of the skills you will probably have acquired:

- How to be an extremely good parent. You will probably be more skilled in this than many parents who haven't had to think so hard about the best way to bring up their children.
- How to feel empathy: you may be better at recognizing other people's problems and suffering, and people may find it very easy to talk to you about these things. You will probably be good at listening to others, and offering support.
- How to think positively: you will have learned how to turn a negative situation into a positive one, and by so doing shape a better future for yourself and your family.

All the above points add up one powerful fact: you will have learned how to be a healing presence in other people's lives as well as your own. This is a real gift, which will make a difference to you and all those you encounter.

The question I leave you with is this: as your children grow up, become more independent and need you less, what are you planning to do with these skills that you've acquired?

There are many ways of using your healing gifts: from little things you think and say each day, to big projects – like organizing parenting workshops or a local support group. Maybe you will find yourself training for a whole new career; only you can recognize the right path for you.

Perhaps you will befriend a parent in your neighbourhood, or a colleague at work who needs support and encouragement. Perhaps you will notice the lack of disabled employees in your place of work, and talk to the right people in personnel to change that situation as soon as possible.

Perhaps you will write your own story and change society's attitudes by so doing. Perhaps you will find some work to do among a particular group of people, like the elderly, the lonely, the homeless or the hungry, all of whom need help.

However you choose to use your skills and experience, good luck. You have earned, through love for your child and endless hard work, the power to make a difference.

Never doubt that you *do* make a difference. Together, we make a noticeable difference. And so, for certain, do our children.

Appendix 1
Useful organizations

Action for Sick Children
300 Kingston Road
London SW20 8LX
Tel: 020 8542 4848
Fax: 020 8542 2424
e-mail: action-for-sick-children-edu@msn.com
Website: www.actionforsickchildren.org.uk

Major UK healthcare charity with many activities, including a national helpline on all aspects of child health care, a specialist library, and a network of local branches providing help, support and information.

American Holistic Medical Association
Tel: (703) 556 9728
Website: www.holisticmedicine.org

Can supply information regarding medical doctors who also practise a natural therapy.

American Osteopathic Association
Tel: (312) 202 8000

Barrington Stoke
10 Belford Terrace
Edinburgh EH4 3DQ
Tel: 0131 315 4933
Fax: 0131 315 4934
e-mail: info@barringtonstoke.co.uk
Website: www.barringtonstoke.co.uk

Specialist publishers of contemporary, very readable books for children and adults who find reading difficult.

Carers National Association
20–25 Glasshouse Yard
London EC1A 4JT
CarersLine: 0345 573 369 (Mon. to Fri., 10 a.m. to midday; 2 p.m. to 4 p.m.)

Ring them for information, advice and free booklets on all aspects of caring, including the publication *Caring for Your Child*, published jointly with Contact a Family (see below), which contains lots of useful addresses, information on benefits, and a guide to all the various experts you may encounter.

Contact a Family
170 Tottenham Court Road
London W1P 0HA
Tel: 020 7383 3555
Website: www.cafamily.org.uk

An excellent source of information about your child's condition, and special needs generally. Ring them for the name and number of the support group that best applies to you and your child, and for helpful free literature (see Carers National Association (above) for the publication *Caring for Your Child*). On Contact a Family's website there is a comprehensive directory of conditions affecting children.

Disability Information Trust
Tel: 01865 227592

Produces a series of useful books on a range of disability subjects. Ring them for a publications brochure.

Disabled Living Foundation
380–384 Harrow Road
London W9 2HU
Tel: 0870 603 9177 (Mon. to Fri., 10 a.m. to 4 p.m.)

Information and advice on disability aids and equipment.

Dyslexia Institute
133 Gresham Road
Staines TW18 2AJ
Tel: 01784 463851
Fax: 01784 460747

Offers advice, information, assessment, teaching and a range of resources (including CD-ROMs) for the 2 million-plus people in the UK who suffer from dyslexia, which can affect reading, writing, spelling and maths skills.

ERIC
Tel: 0117 960 3060

Offers advice over the phone about bedwetting, or can send out a free booklet and leaflets full of ideas and solutions.

Health Information Service
Tel: 0800 66 55 44 (freephone)

Ring the above number for any questions relating to NHS treatment and equipment.

Henry Spink Foundation
170 Tottenham Court Road
London W1P 0HA
Tel: 020 7388 9843
Fax: 020 7387 0342
e-mail: info@henryspink.org
Website: www.info@henryspink.org

An information service set up by a couple who have two children with special needs; this organization can give detailed, unbiased information on a wide range of complementary and other therapies.

La Lèche League
BM 3424
London WC1N 3XX
Tel: 020 7242 1278 (24-hour answerphone)

Can offer help and counselling to mothers with regard to problems in breastfeeding.

National Childbirth Trust (NCT)
Alexandra House
Oldham Terrace
London W3 6NH
Tel: 020 8992 8637

Useful support group for all parents, with branches throughout the UK.
Ring the number above for your local group. They can also offer
advice on issues such as breastfeeding, and can put parents who have
children with medical conditions in touch with one another.

Network 81
1–7 Woodfield Terrace
Stanstead
Essex CM24 8AJ
Helpline: 01279 647 415 (Mon. to Fri., 10 a.m. to 2 p.m.)
For help and advice with statementing and other issues that come under
the Education Act.

Osteopathic Centre for Children
109 Harley Street
London W1N 1DG
Tel: 020 7486 6160

A charity that provides specialist treatment for children at subsidized
rates. Highly popular with parents.

www.our-kids.org/
An excellent starting point for on-line support groups and other
material relating to your child's condition; it is produced by parents for
parents.

Parents for Inclusion
Unit 2
70 South Lambeth Road
London SW8 1RL
Tel: 020 7735 7735
Helpline: 020 7582 5008
e-mail: Pi1@btinternet.com

For help and advice on getting children with special needs into mainstream schools, with support as needed.

RADAR
12 City Forum
250 City Road
London EC1V 8AF
Tel: 020 7250 3222
Fax: 020 7250 0212

Run by, and for, physically disabled people; offers advice over the phone and produces a range of books and booklets on mobility, housing and other disability issues.

TFH
76 Barracks Road
Sandy Lane Industrial Estate
Stourport-on-Severn
Worcestershire DY13 9QB
Tel: 01299 827820
Fax: 01299 827035
e-mail: tfhhq@globalnet.co.uk
Website: www.tfh.com

TFH produces *Fun & Achievement*, a mail order catalogue of toys and equipment for children and adults with special needs. For a free copy, ring TFH (9 a.m. to 9 p.m. seven days a week).

Appendix 2
Help with finance and equipment

There is a lot of financial help available to parents of children with special needs. But knowing what you're entitled to, and how to get it, can be extremely confusing. The following summary should provide you with a good starting point. As a general principle, your health visitor, community paediatrician and other health professionals should be able to point you in the right direction for national and local grants. You can also always get advice, including help with form-filling, from your local Citizens Advice Bureau.

Before you go shopping . . .

Remember that a lot of equipment is available free from your local authority or health service. This includes nappies (for children over the age of three), buggies, wheelchairs, special seating, stair gates, ramps, bath aids and fireguards. In the first instance, ask your health visitor, therapist or other health professional.

Benefits Enquiry Line
Tel: 0800 88 22 00 (freephone)

Ring this number to find out what benefits you are entitled to. They will be able to give you advice on a wide range of benefits, including the two main ones outlined below:

1 *Disability Living Allowance*
   This is not means tested, so every family caring for a child with special needs is eligible. There are several criteria: the most fundamental is that you are caring for a child who needs substantially more help than other children of the same age. Different rates apply according to how much help your child needs. If your child has a terminal condition, special rules apply that help to speed up the process considerably so that you get financial help fast.
2 *Invalid Care Allowance*
   If your child gets Disability Living Allowance above a certain level, and your income falls below certain set limits, you should be eligible for Invalid Care Allowance.

110

The Family Fund Trust
Tel: 01904 621115

This government-funded charity provides financial help for families looking after very disabled children under the age of 16. It also publishes a range of helpful free leaflets on subjects such as adaptations to housing, bedding, benefits checklist, equipment for daily living, holidays, transport, and opportunities for young people after the age of 16.

Family Holiday Association
16 Mortimer Street
London W1N 7RD
Tel: 020 7436 3304

Provides grants for families on a low income for one week's holiday of their choice – usually within Britain. Applications must be made by your health visitor, social worker or health professional.

Local Charities
It's always worth checking, via your health visitor, community paediatrician or other health professional, whether there are grants available from a charity in your neighbourhood.

Appendix 3
Further reading

Many of the books listed below are published in more than one country. In these cases, I've simply mentioned the UK publisher. Quite a few of the books listed are not published in the UK. You can order such titles through a good on-line bookstore such as amazon.co.uk.

Many of the healing books listed focus on healing oneself but, in all cases, exercises can be easily adapted to help your child.

Changed by a Child: Companion Notes for Parents of a Child with a Disability, Barbara Gill, published by Doubleday, New York, USA.
Thoughtful, inspiring collection of short essays that focus on many different aspects of our experiences of special needs.

The Child with Special Needs: Encouraging Intellectual and Emotional Growth, Stanley I. Greenspan MD and Serena Wieder PhD with Robin Simons, published by Perseus Books, Reading, Massachusetts, USA.
This book explains how to understand your child's own particular sensory make-up, and gives excellent insights into how children progress faster when they're motivated by happy feelings. It gives lots of practical ideas on how to help your child progress, and advocates 'floor time', in which you let your child take the lead in play, while you interact with him or her.

Creative Visualization, Shakti Gawain, published by New World Library, Novato, California, USA.
An easy-to-follow guidebook on visualization – a useful beginner's handbook.

Dancing in the Rain: Stories of Exceptional Progress by Parents of Children with Special Needs, edited by Annabel Stehli, published by the Georgiana Organization Inc., Westport, Connecticut, USA.
Inspiring collection of parents' own accounts. It focuses on autism, attention deficit disorder, dyslexia, hyperlexia, communication delay, pervasive developmental delay and similar conditions, and contains detailed accounts of auditory training and its benefits.

The Fragrant Pharmacy: A Complete Guide to Aromatherapy and Essential Oils, Valerie Ann Worwood, published by Bantam Books, London, UK.
A practical, easy-to-use guide to aromatherapy at home.

Hands of Light: A Guide to Healing Through the Human Energy Field, Barbara Ann Brennan, published by Bantam Books, New York, USA.
If you're serious about learning hands-on healing techniques, this is a complete textbook on the subject, written by an ex-NASA physicist who became a counsellor and then a healer.

The Healer Within: Using Traditional Chinese Techniques to Release Your Body's Own Medicine, Roger Jahnke, published by HarperCollins, New York, USA.
Practical guide to movement, massage, meditation and breathing exercises that encourage healing, including advice on how to use the exercises on others.

How to Survive Medical Treatment, Dr Stephen Fulder, published by the C. W. Daniel Co., Saffron Walden, UK.
The philosophy of this book is that it is especially when you are receiving medical treatment that you need a natural health attitude to see you through. Written by a doctor with a holistic outlook, it contains lots of advice on how to get the best out of conventional medicine.

The Intuitive Healer: Accessing Your Inner Physician, Marcia Emery PhD, published by St Martin's Press, New York, USA.
A good workbook for developing your intuition for healing purposes.

Man and His Symbols, Carl Jung, Picador, London, UK.
The classic introduction to understanding your dreams, and using them as a guide to making decisions in your waking life.

The Out-of-Sync Child: Recognizing and Coping with Sensory Integration Dysfunction, Carol Stock Kranowitz MA, published by the Berkeley Publishing Group, New York, USA.
Useful introduction to the subject of sensory processing problems: how to recognize them, and how to help children with them.

The Purpose of Your Life: Finding Your Place in the World Using Synchronicity, Intuition and Uncommon Sense, Carol Adrienne, published by Thorsons, HarperCollins, London, UK.
Many parents find that the experience of having a child with special

needs leads to them reviewing their previous approach to life, and making intuitive changes that seem more in tune with their real selves. For all such people, this is a very helpful book. Two soul-searching questions contained in Chapter 3 of this book were derived from *The Purpose of Your Life*.

Rose Elliot's Vegetarian Cookery, Rose Elliot, published by Harper-Collins, London, UK.
An excellent cook book that gives lots of information about healthy foods, and easy recipes. Of course, you don't have to be vegetarian to enjoy the food! The soup ideas in Chapter 4 of this book were adapted from *Rose Elliot's Vegetarian Cookery*.

Teaching Montessori in the Home: The Pre-school Years, Elizabeth G. Hainstock, published by Penguin Books, New York, USA.
The well-respected Montessori method of teaching young children was originally developed by an Italian doctor, Maria Montessori, for handicapped children. Her techniques recognize the importance of learning through sensory awareness, and through discovering the world for oneself. This book gives simple guidelines to the principles in the home. One of its notable features is the way it focuses on daily household tasks, which young children often enjoy doing with their parents.

Timeless Healing: The Power and Biology of Belief, Herbert Benson MD with Marg Stark, published by Pocket Books, London, UK.
Fascinating book that shows how belief can help healing, while the opposite, which Benson calls the 'nocebo effect', can hinder it.

Why People Don't Heal and How They Can by Caroline Myss PhD, published by Harmony Books/Three Rivers Press, New York, USA.
Best-selling book which says we often see illness as part of someone's identity. That, and a fear of change, explain how individuals can become stuck in illness. This book helps to remove these mental blocks and create the right conditions for health.

Your Baby and Child: The Essential Guide for Every Parent, Penelope Leach, published by Penguin Books, London, UK.
Aimed at parents of all children, this is a great introduction to treating children with respect and understanding, looking at life from their point of view, and helping them to reach their optimum potential.

114

Index

Action for Sick Children, survey 26
acupuncture 73, 75
amazon.co.uk 79
anger 2, 45, 58, 74
antibiotics 85
arnica 33, 85
aromatherapy 32, 65, 75, 79, 81, 85; see also massage
assessment tests 36–7
attention deficit disorder 61
auditory training 61
aura see energy
Austen, Jane 101
autism 61

babysitting, finding the right babysitter 44
Bach flower remedies: Rescue Remedy 33, flower remedies 74, 81, 84
balance, poor sense of see sensory processing problems
behavioural problems 62
Benson, Herbert 30
bonding with your child 3, 11–12
breastfeeding, in hospital 33; discouragement 49
British Medical Journal 25–6, 84
bullying, dealing with 100, 102

cerebral palsy 80
chi see energy
children: your other children 29, 33; considering having another child 52–4
chiropractic 73
choices, giving your child 67
clinginess 74
colour, importance of 32, 66, 86–7
cooking, letting your child help you 71
Coué, Dr Emile 20, 72
comments, dealing with other people's 21–3, 52
communication between you and your child 12
complementary medicine, therapy 11, 17, 27, 60, 61, 62, 73–92
conductive education 61
consultants see doctors
Contact a Family 63, 64, 79
coping strategies 11–23, 30
counselling 40, 44–5
cranial osteopathy see osteopathy
crying 74
crystals 19

decisions, making about your child's health care 56–62
degenerative conditions 9
delayed development 4, 5; see also learning

difficulties
denial 2
depression 58
design, importance of good 68–9
diagnosis 6; lack of 10; getting 24; misdiagnosis 59
dieticians 69
Disability Information Trust 69
Disabled Living Foundation 69
doctors 11, 24–8, 56, 60, 66, 78
Down's Syndrome 6
dreams 17–18

eating problems 13, 35, 62, 69–71
echinacea 84
educational psychologist 96, 100
Einstein, late talking 37, 101
electro-acupuncture 77
emotions: dealing with negative emotions through flower remedies 74; see also feelings
energy, understanding of in complementary therapies, 74–6
epilepsy 22; see also seizures
exercise, importance of 20
expert, yourself as 3; dealing with unhelpful experts 59–60
eye contact, improving 12, 35

failure to thrive 4
family conferences 48
feeding problems see eating problems
feelings: listening to your 38–41, 60; coming to terms with 55–6; getting emotionally stuck 55, 58–9
floor time 12
flower remedies 73; see also Bach flower remedies
friends, coping with 50–1

genes, as art kit 8
genetic condition 5, 7, 9; genetic testing 53–4
GPs see doctors
grandparents 48–50
grommets 15
guilt, feeling 10, 53

hands-on healing see healing
happiness and relaxation 64–7
healing 65, 72, 73, 75, 79, 81; the healer in you 81–92; through prayer 88–9; in visualization 90, 91–2
health visitors 11, 27
Henry Spink Foundation 79–80
Here's Health magazine 79
home remedy kit 84–5
homeopathy 33, 73, 74, 76–8, 79, 84, 85
hospital 28–34
'hospital at home' treatment 31

hypotonia 22

IEP (individual education plan) 99
immunity, raising a child's 70, 75, 84, 88
inclusive education 64, 95; *see also* schools
Indian head massage 75, 81
insurance, medical 80

Journal of the American Medical Association 40

kinesiology 73, 75

La Lèche League 33
language, choosing words to suit you 22
laughter: barometer of coping 42; importance of 65, 66, 86
Law of Concentrated Attention 72
learning difficulties, delays 4, 5, 39, 61
life: living it to the full 9, 56; fears about life expectancy 10
listening, importance of 47
Liszt 101

massage 32, 43, 87
medical tests 24–5, 32
meditation 20, 66, 75
messiness, importance of letting a child get messy 71
microcephaly 5, 93
Microcephaly Support Group 93
mobility equipment 62, 68
motivation, child's 8
music, value of 14, 65; in hospital 33

National Childbirth Trust 33
nightmares 74
nocebo effect 30

occupational therapy 17, 24, 34, 69
on-line support groups 62–3
Osteopathic Centre for Children 81
osteopathy 73, 75, 76–8, 79, 80

Parents for Inclusion 96
partner, your relationship with your 41–6
penpal clubs, for siblings 48
physiotherapy 13, 17, 24, 34
playing with your child 12, 29, 33, 47–8, 66
portage 17, 35
positive affirmations 20–1, 30
potential, your child's 9
prana *see* energy
probiotics 71, 85
proprioceptive receptors 16

quadriplegia 93

questions to ask doctors 30

rainbows: making 47–8; rainbow colours in healing 86, 91
reflexology 73, 75, 79, 81, 87
reiki 75
relaxation *see* happiness
repetitive movements 16
rest: importance of 87–8; *see also* 'hospital at home' treatment
Rimsky-Korsakov 101

sad, feeling 10, 53, 74
scared, feeling 10
schools 20, 57, 87, 93, 94, 95–7
seizures 80; *see also* epilepsy
SENCO (special educational needs co-ordinator) 99
sensitivity to touch, sound etc. *see* sensory processing problems
sensory integration therapy *see* sensory processing problems
sensory processing problems 5, 13–17, 23, 34, 51, 61, 74, 76–7
shiatsu 75
shock 2, 24
siblings 46–8, 53; *see also* children
skin brushing 17, 34
sleep problems 62
soups 70
special schools 95; *see also* schools
speech therapy 17, 24, 35, 69
statementing, statement of special educational needs 37–8, 96, 97–100
Stehli, Annabel 61
steroids 84
support groups 40–1, 48, 49–50, 54, 60, 62–4
synaesthesia 101

talking, importance 43, 45, 50, 93; *see also* listening
tests *see* assessment tests and medical tests
therapists 11, 34; *see also* physiotherapy, occupational therapy, speech therapy, portage
toddler tantrums 74
toilet training 62
toxoplasmosis 77
trauma, minimizing your child's 29
Tripp Trapp chair by Stokke 69

vestibular receptors 16
visualization 46, 75, 82, 89–92

yoga 75, 81, 82